Praise for *The Upside of Disruption*

"Breakthrough thinking to unlock huge potential."

—Chris Barton,
Founder of Shazam

"Terence Mauri's work is always required reading for all who know the value of great leadership. This book is no exception. It is a game changer."

—Stuart Crainer,
Co-founder of Thinkers50

"Terence's work captures the opportunities of change by replacing fear with hope, uncertainty with certainty, ambivalence with action, and doubt with confidence; all of which are more needed today than ever!"

—Dave Ulrich,
Rensis Likert Professor,
Ross School of Business University of Michigan

"A no-nonsense playbook for leaders navigating the new normal with confidence and creativity."

—Michele Zanini,
co-author of *Humanocracy*

"Buckle up! The Upside of Disruption *will take you and your mindset for a ride as Terence presents new ways of thinking, doing, and believing."*

—Grace Chen,
Quantic School of Business and Technology

"A timely book that helps us understand the true value of disruptive ideas."

—Tomas Chamorro-Premuzic,
Professor of Business Psychology at UCL and Columbia

"Navigating uncertainty has become business-as-usual, and despite the human instinct to seek stability, leaders and companies need to demonstrate curiosity and courage and decide on strategies where the outcome is not always predictable. Terence Mauri is a great change-maker and thought-provoker who gets us all to embrace change. The Upside of Disruption *is a great guide to that mindset."*

—Anders Dons,
Nordic CEO, Deloitte

"The Upside of Disruption: *A wake-up call from the future. It's up to us to act now."*

—Yannick Theler,
CEO of Steer Studios

"A new book by Terence Mauri is a fresh boost to my ideas and understanding. It is disruptive in an entirely good way. He is in a class of his own when narrating the future of leadership."

—Julia Hobsbawm OBE,
futurist of work, Bloomberg commentator,
and author of Working Assumptions

"With The Upside of Disruption, *Terence Mauri shows that a new age of business requires a new approach to leadership. To understand the new era, read this book."*

—Richard Straub,
Founder and President,
Global Peter Drucker Forum

"Terence's book is a laser-sharp read, designed to captivate you into the agility journey!"

—Dr. Mark Esposito,
Co-founder at Nexus FrontierTech
and Professor of Economics,
Strategy, and Foresights at
Hult International Business School

"In this world of perpetual transformation often accelerated by uncertainty and disruption, this vital book is your companion for action. Read it and act on it!"
—Tahirou Assane Oumarou,
Director of Brightline at PMI

"As change will be the new normal, we need to get comfortable with constant change and the unknown to be healthy and successful. Terence's bold vision of 'the upside of disruption' is a blueprint for agility and adaptability."
—Marga Hoek,
Author of *Tech for Good: Solving the World's Greatest Challenges*

"This much-needed book is brimming with insights, especially in what is at the core of ALL change – the right mindset. Tools and tech certainly enable or ignite change, but none will be used to its advantage without our approach, attitude, and vision."

—Abigail Posner,
Director, Creative Works at Google

"This is the book every leader needs to read. Embracing disruption rather than combatting it. In one word: 'Brilliant!'
—Friederike Fabritius,
Neuroscientist and
Wall Street Journal bestselling author

"It's an essential read! Rigorously researched and powerfully imagined, Terence Mauri has masterfully provided a comprehensive, insightful, and intellectually stimulating formula for thriving in the unknown. In these disruptive times, business leaders can gain a competitive edge by turning risks into opportunities. Don't head into the future without The Upside of Disruption.*"*
—Frank-Jürgen Richter,
Founder and Chairman, Horasis

"*A must-read for those who want to become future fit leaders today!*"

—Steve Hamilton,
Partner & Chief Coaching Officer,
The Henka Institute

"*Many talk about adapting to change, but few can succinctly capture the* why *and* how. *Terence Mauri does both in this groundbreaking new book, which is a must-read for innovative leaders.*"

—Ruchika Tulshyan,
author of *Inclusion on Purpose*

"*Brimming with insights,* The Upside of Disruption *shows us that successful adaptation isn't just about tech and trends, it's about mindsets.*"

—Dan Cable,
author of *Alive at Work: The Neuroscience of Helping Your People Love What They Do*

"*In an era of disruption, adapting is the only viable strategy. Terence Mauri explains how to do exactly that in this wonderful book!*"

—Greg Satell,
Co-founder of ChangeOS and Wharton Business School lecturer

"*Leaders need to seek out fresh perspectives and embrace new mindsets to thrive in the future. Terence Mauri shows you how.* The Upside of Disruption *proposes an urgent agenda of actions leaders must take to turn uncertainty into action.*"

—Kaihan Krippendorff,
Founder of Outthinker Networks; bestselling
author of Driving Innovation from Within

"*From dislocated supply chains to financial crises, geopolitical shifts to wars and pandemics, uncertainty is today's only business certainty. But as Terence Mauri reminds us in this important book, it isn't all doom and gloom. Silver linings and tailwinds exist for those prepared to seize the opportunities and manage the threats. Brimming with insights,* The Upside of Disruption *is an indispensable guide to surviving and thriving in our new topsy-turvy reality.*"

—Des Dearlove,
Co-founder of Thinkers50

"*A playbook to turn disruption into action, drive strategy, and elevate your talent and leadership.*"

—Peter Fisk,
Academic Director of IE Business School
and Founder of GeniusWorks

"*What if we re-frame disruption as a real possibility to reinvent ourselves? Terence Mauri's new book provides a compelling framework with storytelling that will help you see the opportunities unfolding here and now in front of us. Not to be missed.*"

—Paolo Gallo,
author and former Chief Human Resources
Officer at the World Economic Forum

"*Disruption is ubiquitous and affects everyone with unseen speed. Leaders who believe they should not learn and unlearn will soon find themselves at an irreversible disadvantage.* The Upside of Disruption, *therefore, is indispensable for leaders who want to own the future!*"

—Katja Schipperheijn,
Founder of Habit Improvement

"*Adaptation is how we have always survived. Mauri gives us all a vision of something greater than simple survival. By changing our mindsets, we change the game and can pre-adapt our thinking to the future, allowing us to scale a bolder, brighter, better future for all.*"

—Dr. Rebecca Heiss,
CEO and Founder of Icueity

"*Terence Mauri's* The Upside of Disruption *masterfully transforms the chaos of change into a landscape of opportunity. It's a brave wake-up call for leaders eager to navigate the new with agility and foresight.*"

—Benjamin Laker,
author and Professor of Leadership and
Director of Impact and Global Engagement
at Henley Business School

"*It's a thought-provoking guide for leaders to transform disruption into strategic courage and navigate the unknown with adaptability, boldness, and a winning mindset.*"

—Artur Smejlis,
Founder of Everyday Development

"*Extreme times are also extreme catalyzers of inner strength and determination.* The Upside of Disruption *walks with you into the unknown and illuminates a way forward through actions that fire you up to succeed, not despite adversity, but, in fact, because of it.*"

—E. Elisabet Lahti, Ph.D.,
Founder of Sisu Lab, Author of
*Gentle Power: A Revolution in How We Think,
Lead and Succeed Using the Finnish Art of Sisu*

"*Terence Mauri's* The Upside of Disruption *is an indispensable guide for leaders seeking to transform disruption into opportunity. Terence doesn't just understand the dynamics of change; he translates it into actionable strategies that empower us to lead with agility and confidence. I've seen his principles in action, and they are as transformative as they are vital for success in an era that demands adaptability. This book is a catalyst for bold thinking and brave choices, essential for anyone who aspires to shape the future rather than be shaped by it.*"

—Rachel Treece,
CEO of Henka Institute

"In the unchartered waters of today's world, where change is the only constant, one of the biggest mistakes leaders can make is pretending they know more than they do or making decisions relying only on their instinct or previous experience. Leadership is first being, then doing. From my perspective, the cornerstone of being a bold leader is self-awareness, including examining every blind spot, learning about your biases, beliefs, and triggers, and – most importantly – taking responsibility for your BS. A much-needed book for these times."

—Monique Borst,
CEO, catalyst, strategist, and coach

"It's easy to feel stuck in the constant uncertainty and complexity of the post-pandemic world. Mauri presents a compelling vision of becoming unstuck. The Upside of Disruption *is an indispensable guide to moving forward boldly on a personal and organizational level.*"

—Dr. Steven MacGregor,
Author of *Chief Wellbeing Officer* and *The Daily Reset*

THE UPSIDE OF DISRUPTION

About Thinkers50

Thinkers50 is the world's most reliable resource for identifying, ranking, and sharing the leading management and business ideas of our age. Since 2001, we've been providing access to ideas with the power to make a positive difference in the world.

The Thinkers50 definitive ranking of management thinkers is published every two years. Its Distinguished Achievement Awards, which recognize the very best in management thinking and practice, have been described by the Financial Times as the "Oscars of management thinking."

TERENCE MAURI

THE UPSIDE OF DISRUPTION

THE PATH TO LEADING AND THRIVING IN THE UNKNOWN

WILEY

Library of Congress Cataloging-in-Publication Data

Names: Mauri, Terence, author. | John Wiley & Sons, publisher.
Title: The upside of disruption : the path to leading and thriving in the
   unknown / Terence Mauri.
Other title: Thinkers50 (John Wiley & Sons)
Description: Hoboken, New Jersey : Wiley, [2024] | Includes index.
Series: Thinkers50 series
Identifiers: LCCN 2024014714 (print) | LCCN 2024014715 (ebook) | ISBN
   9781394192601 (hardback) | ISBN 9781394192618 (adobe pdf) | ISBN
   9781394193639 (epub)
Subjects: LCSH: Leadership. | Success in business. | Organizational change.
Classification: LCC HD57.7 .M39349 2024 (print) | LCC HD57.7 (ebook) |
   DDC 658.4/092—dc23/eng/20240506
LC record available at https://lccn.loc.gov/2024014714
LC ebook record available at https://lccn.loc.gov/2024014715

Cover Design: Wiley
Cover Image: © t_kimura/Getty Images
Author Photo: Courtesy of Terence Mauri
SKY10079492_071724

To Polona Pirnat

Contents

Chapter 1	A Wake-up Call from the Future	1
	Leadership on the Ballot	5
	Future-ready Mindsets	7
	Questions Are the Answer	14
	Don't Mention the 'D' Word	16
	Disruption Is the Norm; the Upside Is a Choice	17
	The Upside Is the Answer	18
	The Nutritional Value of Leadership	21
Chapter 2	Data: Lead with AI	31
	Leadership Disrupted	35
	Making the Impossible Possible	36
	Amazonification Principles	38
	The Most Significant Risk Is Not AI	39
	Underhyped Versus Overhyped	40
	A Brief History of AI	42
	The AI-Intelligence Illusion	47
	Attention Is the New Oil	50
	Matching AI with Leadership and Humanity	54
	The Anything Workforce	55
	Be a Future-maker	60
	Takeaways	61

Chapter 3   Agility: Great Leaders Unlearn   65
                  Learning for Today While Unlearning
                        for Tomorrow   68
                  Mind the Agility Gap   71
                  Slow, Siloed, and Complicated   74
                  Measure My Bureaucratic BS (Score Yourself
                        on a Scale of 1–5) 5 = "Strongly Agree"   75
                  Failure to Reimagine Failure   79
                  A Brief History of Failure   81
                  From Action, I Learn (FAIL)   84
                  A Story of Unlearning a Toxic Culture   87
                  Unlearning Is the Answer   92
                  Unlearning Equals Agility and Humility   95
                  Takeaways   96

Chapter 4   Risk: The Courage Advantage   101
                  The Courage Dividend   108
                  Courage Calling   108
                  Willful Contrarianism   115
                  The Mindset Advantage   120
                  The Beyonders   122
                  Wanted – Leaders of Courage   127
                  Takeaways   127

Chapter 5   Evolution: In Trust, We Grow   133
                  Truth Decay in Organizations   136
                  Trust on the Ballot   136
                  Trust in Humans   137
                  Trust Decay   139
                  The Trust Mindset   142
                  Believing   146
                  Belonging   146
                  Braving   147
                  Becoming   148

	Who We Are Is What We Do	148
	The Future of Trust	157
	Trust Is The Ultimate Human Currency	164
	Takeaways	165

Chapter 6   Beyond Is Where We Begin   169

First, When Disruption Is the Norm, Rethinking Is the Answer   171

Second, Technology Changes Fast. Humans Don't   173

Third, In the Human-Technology Nexus, Courage Skills Are the New Leadership   175

Beware of the Rubber Band Effect   177

The Dogs That Don't Bark   179

Frontier Leadership   180

Chapter 7   The DARE Leadership Test   187

Data   189

Agility   190

Risk   190

Evolution   190

Notes   191

Acknowledgments   209

About the Author   211

Index   213

1

A Wake-up Call from the Future

"You can't use an old map to explore a new world."

– Albert Einstein

Not too long ago, I experienced the future by letting a driverless car navigate me through the streets of San Francisco. I was on a business trip and staying at a hotel in downtown Union Square. I'd read a lot about Google's spin-off Waymo and General Motors's subsidiary Cruise to operate 24/7 hail-riding services in the city and was curious to test one out. Rumor has it that the cars cost more than $200,000.00 each and are fitted with hundreds of high sensors and cameras to ensure a safe ride.[1] I didn't know what to expect and felt nervous, but as somebody who writes and speaks about the future, I always try to embrace new experiences, even life-or-death ones. I first decided to get a coffee for a good dose of courage and opened the Waymo app, just like Uber or Lyft. My destination was a well-known restaurant where San Francisco's Golden Gate Park meets the Pacific Ocean. I pressed "go," and a message alerted me that my Waymo ride was on its way and that it would take around nine minutes to arrive outside my hotel. Still drinking my coffee, I followed my ride as it approached the hotel and waited with a mix of fear and excitement. A few moments later, I watched as a gleaming white Jaguar pulled up on the other side of the road with its distinctive Waymo logo on the side.

My first reaction was embarrassment as people nearby started staring at the car, and I was tempted to cancel the ride immediately. The writer Hilary Mantel said, "The question is not who influences you, but which people give you courage." It takes courage to step into the unknown, but FOMO (Fear of Missing Out) is also a powerful motivator; it is always easier when you don't overthink.

The ancient Stoics were right. "Do faster than doubt," I said to myself. As I walked across the road, I could feel my heart racing. I reached for the door handle, but it wouldn't open. I could feel the stares fixated on my next move. I needed to press the "unlock" button on the app, and the handles came out of the door so I could climb inside. "Hello, Trip," a voice said through the car's speakers. "Please don't touch the steering wheel or pedals during the ride. For any questions, you can find information in the Waymo app, like how we keep our cars safe or clean." As my ride pulled away, a pedestrian gave the car and me a scared look and said, "WTF." I felt the same. As the future happens faster than ever, there is fear and excitement, but is enough being done by leaders to seize the future boldly because technology changes quickly, but humans don't?

"NOBODY KNOWS WHAT'S GOING TO HAPPEN."

Sam Altman, CEO of OpenAI, has a sign above his desk that reads, "Nobody knows what is going to happen."[2] This could be the headline news for leaders today as they grapple with multiplying disruptions in AI, geopolitical risk, wars in Ukraine and the Middle East, talent shortages, and industry convergence. It's disruption everywhere and all at once and shocks upon shocks. With economic headwinds and tech disruption an everyday reality, we should not waste one of the most significant reframing moments because the future isn't just about technology and trends. It's about mindsets and choices, too. Zombie leadership, where dead management ideas live on, and the curse of sameness are seductive leadership biases. Knowing serves us well in a linear, predictable, and stable world. It is radically different today: the compounding effect of extreme disruption, difficult-to-predict challenges, and high-velocity contexts can't be solved with yesterday's mindsets or assumptions. Filtering through hype cycles for business relevance matters, too. As a result, we suffer from collective future blindness, held captive to strategies of similarity and leadership models that, at best, can be described as "over-managed" and "under-led."[3]

Leadership on the Ballot

- 93% of leaders expect significant AI-driven disruption over the next five years, but only 27% have the right mindsets and capabilities to respond
- 81% of leaders agree that they feel overwhelmed by the speed and scale of business disruption
- 77% of leaders believe that their organizations suffer from talent-crushing bureaucracy
- 64% of leaders agree that their future readiness muscle is an obstacle to boldly seizing the future
- 59% of leaders agree their organizations prioritize control and efficiency instead of agility and intelligence
- 51% of leaders agree they don't have enough time in their day to achieve their must-do priorities

Source: Hack Future Lab

Leadership is broken, and the data tells the story. As reported in Gallup, 6 in 10 employees worldwide aren't engaged at work, and only 20% of US workers say "they have a best friend at work."[4] Today's leaders suffer from record levels of distraction, overload, and worry about the future, and their teams are disengaged and tired. AI and job automation, talent scarcity, and cost constraints expose organizations to a culture of SEP – "Somebody Else's Problem" – a broken work-place of excuses, back-covering, and inertia. They call it "Tang Ping" in China, which means protesting against work by lying on your back, a fate we must avoid at all costs.[5]

"How does the future happen? Gradually, then suddenly," to paraphrase the writer Ernest Hemingway.[6] I was born in the early 1970s. My first "home computer" had 1k of RAM and played the Space Invaders game, which was as good as the arcade version. Monochrome only, but so was the arcade game. A few years later, I persuaded my parents to upgrade to a Commodore 64 called the C-64. I played games like Wizball and Mission Impossible, which would take half an hour to load on cassette players and make a screeching noise. Often, seconds before loading the game was complete, something would go wrong, and a "syntax error" message would pop up in the middle of the screen. I loved it. It was a slower, predictable world over today's rapid, fluid one. Fast-forward to today's age of AI. Project December is an AI tool that can simulate conversations with anyone, including the dead.[7]

Project December promises to "create realistic text-based conversation" with our departed loved ones; the next iteration will be a voice-based AI chatbot with the option to sound like anyone you know or have known who has sadly died. The phrase "Fortune favors the bold" is a translation of a Latin proverb, "Audentes Fortuna Luvat," and a timely reminder of a leader's mindset to be ready to adapt to anything, however unusual.[8] Future-readiness is a mindset that prepares you for the unthinkable. When operating at the edge of a new world, we must rethink old certainties, search for the upside, and ask what will evolve and what will *not* change because the untapped value lies there, too.

The upside of disruption is waiting to be discovered. All we have to do is stop and listen. Yet, many leaders suffer the equivalent of "cognitive shock" grappling with the twin demands of leading for today while managing for tomorrow and suspended between the comforts of the past and the possibilities of the future. Hack Future Lab's research shows this isn't very surprising, considering most leaders (91%) expect technology to continue as a primary business disruptor, followed by rising customer expectations (83%) and industry convergence (74%).[9]

As disruption accelerates and business models decay faster, leaders are tested in terms of future readiness and organizational resilience: they must stop, flip the switch, turn on the lights, and see and ask what's up ahead without fear and ask – "How do I lead the future with clarity and fortitude?"

Future-ready Mindsets

Future readiness is only as good as our mindsets, choices, and assumptions. It's time to upend the assumption that leaders are the preservers of the status quo; we are the challengers of the status quo. I believe a change in perspective is worth at least 100 IQ points because our current perceptions are grounded in our past assumptions. The Philosopher Yuk Hui wrote, "To regain the future, we must nurture our relationship with the unknown."[10] Every business starts as an act of disruption, but to sustain vitality for the long term requires reimagination, which is the human force that can push through the unknown and define a bolder future. New contexts demand fresh perspectives because today's leadership models don't support what's coming next. A series of disruptive trends threaten to upend and reshape every industry over the next five years – AI, industry convergence, talent scarcity, new customers, new regulations, and new competitors will only accelerate.

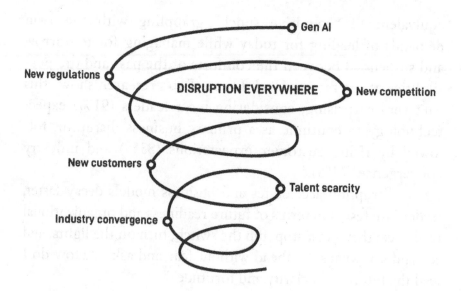

1. Generative AI

Accelerated computing and generative AI have hit the tipping point, with demand surging worldwide across companies, industries, and nations. AI's impact is set to revolutionize every facet of our lives, encompassing leadership, work, creativity, and competition. We are experiencing the Age of Co-intelligence, where humans will leverage AI as a co-thinker to solve problems, spark creativity, and make decisions. The disruptions we witness today are merely the start. AI possesses two exceptional capabilities: generating new ideas and concepts independently and making decisions autonomously. This will reshape our perception of intelligence and productivity, creating new synergies and human-to-machine collaborative teamwork. While tasks will be accomplished at an unprecedented speed, the implications extend beyond hyper-efficiency. AI ushers in a new era of humans and machines, empowering employees with super-human abilities such as speed to insights, innovation driven by anomalies, and the power to assimilate early-to-exploit contexts before others. Leaders must learn to leverage this era of co-intelligence to operate as a human-centric, AI-enabled frontier organization.

2. Industry convergence

Industry convergence is the ultimate goal for thriving firms worldwide, and any traditional business aiming to stay competitive must prioritize this trend. As firms accelerate their AI and cloud transformations, they should consider three main horizons to capture more value from cross-industry synergies: digitizing their core operations, expanding into adjacent services to serve customers better, and embracing industry convergence. The movie Blackberry shows a team of clever inventors too love-struck with their iconic keyboard to realize that Apple had reinvented its entire market; Apple could threaten any industry next through its continuous reinvention and refinement strategy.[11]

Today, a winner-takes-all effect occurs from industry convergence whereby 90% of economic profit is earned by the top 10% of firms by market capitalization.[12] The most valuable firms own the most valuable algorithms: the MAANMA companies (Microsoft, Apple, Amazon, NVIDIA, Meta, and Alphabet) have a combined enterprise value of $8 trillion, accounting for more than 22% of the S&P 500's index weighting and nearly half of the Nasdaq-100 index.[13] Everything and everyone is connected now. Industry convergence boosted by network effects, economies of scale, and speed of disruption means that Amazon, for example, could easily disrupt the $1 trillion drug distribution market through its "Everything Store."

In Europe, the winner-takes-all effect is happening too, with 11 companies known as the "GRANOLAS" driving European stocks to historic peaks, mirroring the famous

"MAANMA" in the United States. Goldman Sachs created this catchy acronym for GSK, Roche, ASML, Nestlé, Novartis, Novo Nordisk, L'Oréal, LVMH, AstraZeneca, SAP, and Sanofi. The big keeps getting bigger, powered by mergers, AI, and wide and deep moats.[14]

3. Talent scarcity

In Ancient Greece, talent was a unit of currency; today, our future readiness strategy is only as good as our skills and talent.[15] Leadership's mantra for managing disruption could be "Talent, talent, talent." Talent is one of the best ways to outpace the forces of AI and industry disruption, and leaders boast, "Our talent is our greatest asset," yet the war for talent is over. Talent won. Fear and hysteria are at peak levels when managing talent scarcity. We have The Great Resignation (record levels of employees quitting their jobs) and The Big Quit, a term coined by Professor Anthony Klotz.[16] The Hybrid Paradox (what's our workforce hybrid strategy?) and the Race to Reskill (one of the best ways to outpace the forces of disruption is upskilling and reskilling). It's no wonder 80% of leaders report high levels of concern about intensifying workforce turnover and talent risk.[17] The World Economic Forum has estimated that up to 90% of the global working population will need to reskill and upskill by 2030 to meet the demands of a post-industrial AI-centric economy. A failure to do so could cost as much as $15 trillion in lost GDP. Leaders have a huge role in tackling the talent scarcity gap and building inclusive, resilient, talent-led futures.[18]

4. New customers

In today's hyper-connected world, new customers demand that firms provide intuitive and connected moments that matter at every interaction. It's personalization at light speed: the right person, right time, right message, and proper context.

The global pandemic, which was dubbed a "time machine from the future," accelerated business trends and the transformation of entire industries at the speed of Moore's Law, named after the engineer who observed that a computer processing chip doubles every 18 months: e-commerce, automation, remote work, and business models were digitized and reimagined, and change became horizontal and universal.[19] Every day, we read about iconic firms failing to learn at the speed of the customer, from Disney and Peloton to Charles Schwab and Chevron.[20]

Firms that fall behind in their industry have not suddenly become stupid or made the wrong bet on the future? Leaders are trapped in leadership mindsets of conformity that are hardwired to reject ideas that challenge the status quo over mindsets of courage that embrace ideas that challenge the status quo. While we all want our organizations to grow, we must accept that "finding the upside in disruption" is the most important (and challenging) issue for leaders today. Push too hard, and panic ensues. Take it too easy; you're in the conformity zone – a no-go for growth. As leaders, it's our job to model courage over conformity, where others can discover the upside in disruption and turn it into opportunity.

Liquid Death is a water brand with the tagline "Murder Your Thirst" that has a market valuation of more than $500 million from when it was founded in 2019 by Mike Cessario. Let's face it: Water is boring, and yet Liquid Death's meteoric rise makes the firm more than a provocative name. "At the end of the day, we're creating an entertainment company and a water company," says Cessario, where search and entertainment recommendations will become increasingly personalized and algorithmically driven.[21] New customers want products and services that aren't just functional; they want meaning and to feel connected to a shared purpose, what the late psychiatrist Oliver Sachs called the three Bs: Bonding, Belonging, and Becoming.[22]

5. New competitors

It's no longer just about big or small. It's about fast or slow. Scale is an advantage until it's not. Take note of the recent swath of demergers (General Electric, Johnson & Johnson, and Toshiba). Activist investors such as Value Act, Engine No. 1, and Third Point are fighting proxy battles, keeping CEOs awake at night (e.g., consider the proxy battle won by Engine No. 1 to appoint independent directors on the board of Exxon Mobil). When the world changes, we must respond with fortitude and have the capacity to embrace continuous evolution.[23]

Disruption always presents leaders with a choice of: 1. Opportunity and renewal if the upside of disruption is harnessed as a *tailwind* or 2. Relapse and decline if disruption is perceived as a headwind or dismissed as a "blip" in the market. Sometimes, disruption isn't easy to spot. Steve Ballmer, co-founder of Microsoft, famously said that Apple's new iPhone was a waste of money: "Five hundred dollars? A big glass screen and fully subsidized?"[24] We know what happened next. Disruption and its closest cousin, courage, have given leaders a once-in-a-lifetime opportunity to rethink the new logic of competition. Leaders are now competing on the speed of learning, physical and digital platforms, talent and resiliency, and speed to insights through AI as co-thinkers. The next 10 years will continue to scale exponentially, upending entire industries and reshaping existing ones with more than $60 trillion of enterprise value at risk of disruption.[25] Will you watch the world change around you, or will you be the one leading the disruption from the inside?

6. New regulations

The megatrends of decarbonization and AI-driven disruption are converging and compounding, creating unprecedented risk and cross-industry regulatory pressures for leaders. The $740 billion Inflation Reduction Act is a transformative law that supercharges global energy transition into renewables and increases demand for green technologies. On the other side of the pond, the EU is introducing a Corporate Sustainability Reporting Directive, and Scope 3 emissions is a new regulatory requirement, too.[26] Together, they will help reduce emissions across the supply chain and sustain a firm's sustainability and decarbonization journey as we risk exceeding 1.5 degrees Celsius of warming by 2040.[27]

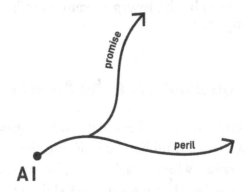

The perils of blindly relying on technology without adequate guardrails have also been demonstrated. Elon Musk is suing Open AI, the makers of ChatGPT, arguing that its commercial deal with Microsoft has broken the firm's mission to build "artificial intelligence" for humanity.[28] This lawsuit raises crucial concerns about whether AI will prioritize financial gains over ethical considerations because striking a delicate balance between innovation and regulatory oversight is a must for the long-term success of AI. Regulatory bodies like the US Securities Exchange Commission

(SEC), led by chair Gary Gensler, are already expressing concerns about data protection, antitrust issues, and market stability. Leaders must, therefore, replace overconfidence with humility to resist the allure of AI's rapid advancement.[29]

The current regulatory landscape is at a tipping point. Leaders must prioritize trust, transparency, and ethical algorithms to embrace AI's promise fully. This means regulating companies without stifling innovation and adopting an ethics-first approach driven by human values. Actively participating in the co-development of new regulations and guidelines is crucial for unlocking the upside of AI. For instance, Mustafa Suleyman, the founder of Inflection AI, advocates for creating an International Panel on AI Safety (IPAIS) inspired by the Intergovernmental Panel on Climate Change (IPCC).[30]

Questions Are the Answer

The late Professor Richard Feynman said, "Knowledge is having the right answers. Intelligence is asking the right questions. Wisdom is knowing when to ask the right questions."[31] Questions sharpen two vastly underutilized skill sets: courage and humility. To find the upside in disruption, we must be willing to step out from a world of familiarity to a world of possibility where the reward is surprising but helpful insights and new opportunities for breakthrough growth and game-changing ideas. Questions are central to finding the upside in disruption and are the key to shifting from a "yes, but" mindset to a "yes, and?" one.

What are the boldest questions you will ask this year that won't just make you feel good but make you think hard? If you stop for four minutes a day to ask new questions, that's 24 hours of further questions a year. Questions are the key to unlocking the door to thinking differently about the future. I was in a media interview midway through, and a particular pattern caught my attention. Every question the interviewer asked me began with the word "but." It almost felt like my words were being brushed aside, making way for a new question that aimed to catch me off guard. The *Improv Handbook* by Deborah Frances-White and Tom Salinsky explores the significance of saying "yes" to new ideas and embracing the unknown with wonder. They emphasize that this act of acceptance carries a certain degree of risk. We must assume new and unfamiliar worlds and allow them to shape our thinking. While saying "yes, but" may provide a sense of certainty and security, saying "yes, and" encourages us to take a courageous leap into the future and discover the upside of disruption.[32]

"YES, BUT"   VS   **"YES, AND"**

Here are a series of questions to start becoming a "Yes, and" leader and cultivate a collective mindset of willingness and humility to change from within.

- What are our billion-dollar beliefs (e.g., AI, decarbonization, sustainability) about the future?
- Are we protecting and prioritizing our billion-dollar beliefs? If not, why not?
- What's enduring, emerging, and eroding in our leadership?
- Which mindsets and assumptions about the future are going untested and why?
- Do we intentionally sharpen our future readiness muscle, exploring and exploiting the upside of disruption, or take a "wait and see" approach?

- As the rate of disruption accelerates, do we have a collective unlearning strategy to eliminate the "always-done ways" and stay ahead of the speed of change?

- What future "success headlines" do we want to be written about us?

- Do we have the right mindsets, cultures, and capabilities to sustain the above?

Don't Mention the 'D' Word

The word disruption has been mentioned more than 2,500 times in quarterly earnings calls in the last three months. The self-proclaimed Economist of Doom, Nouriel Roubini, has identified 10 "D"s driving the 2020s: Debt, Deflation, Depression, Deficits, Demographics, Decarbonization, De-globalization, Democratic Backlash, Digitization, and Deadly Disasters, e.g., The Global Pandemic.[33]

Like most words in the business lexicon, disruption has lost its meaning. Disruption means both change and opportunity. It's something that can shake up the status quo for better or for worse. I want to reject the false constraint that disruption always happens to leaders and their organizations. The history of humanity is a history of steep learning curves, difficult choices, and periods of profound crises. Stone Age, Bronze Age, Iron Age, and now the Age of AI, automation, and analytics. Did you know that most of today's famous hectocorns ($100 billion Equity Market Valuations) were born from a crisis (e.g., Square, Inc., Airbnb, and Uber were all launched during the Global Financial Crisis of 2008-2009) and iconic companies such as UPS, Volvo, and HP were started more than a hundred years ago during The Great Depression? By responding to disruption with action, companies can adapt, thrive, and drive positive change in their industries and beyond.[34]

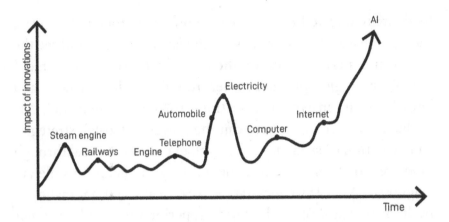

Disruption Is the Norm; the Upside Is a Choice

- 100,000 years ago, we harnessed fire, which led to language
- 10,000 years ago, we developed agriculture and commerce, which led to the marketplace
- 5,000 years ago, we invented writing and the wheel, which led to travel and cities
- 175 years ago, we witnessed The Industrial Revolution and its vast economic impact from innovation platforms such as electricity, automobiles, and the telephone

Today, innovation platforms such as Blockchain, energy storage, AI, robotics, and DNA sequencing are converging in ways that will create massive shifts in the logic of competition, the nature of work, and the role of leadership. Companies associated with these innovation platforms increased their equity market capitalizations by more than $5.1 trillion in one year, and the next 10 years will continue to scale exponentially, upending entire industries and value chains and reshaping existing ones.[35]

Some pioneer firms are already embracing the upside of disruption with early-to-exploit strategies such as Forever Beta, Co-lab, and Minimum Viable Idea (MVI). Forever Beta strategies can be observed in products like FitBit or Tesla, which can be digitally updated to the cloud, allowing customers to update their purchases continuously with the latest software and see the utility and performance of their product grow over time.[36] Co-lab strategies produce faster results in the sciences and knowledge-intensive organizations through human-led, AI-enabled discovery. Nowhere can the power of Co-lab strategies and execution be seen more clearly than the recent breakthrough blood test that can predict dementia 15 years before people are diagnosed. MVI strategies target weak leaks and anomalies in traditional industries and provide superior value and customer service. Revolut, an upstart online bank, combines AI chatbots, the cloud, and machine learning to create powerful new engines of value creation and difficult-to-copy customer insights.[37]

The Upside Is the Answer

I started thinking about the idea for *The Upside of Disruption* after the pandemic. At the time, I was traveling and speaking extensively to global business audiences about how leaders often miss the upside of disruption because they are overwhelmed by relentless change and lack the right leadership mindsets to lean into the unknown. When we crave the comfort of certainty, it creates fear of the unknown and is a barrier to learning and growth. The upside of disruption is rooted in courage and the belief that the best is yet to come. It creates possibility in the unknown and is a hedge against a risk-averse mindset. The problem starts with traditional leadership theories that are often rooted in the belief that we can effectively plan and predict our future. However, today's leaders are confronted with a different reality. Scarring from a series of geopolitical and economic shocks generates a risk-averse mindset that is holding back leaders, and yet I would argue that an uncertain world needs to take on more risk to avoid collective caution.

This "paradox of risk" - in seeking to avoid risks, we amplify them is compounded by a need for sustainable courage skills (pro-change, pro-growth and proactive), leaving leaders and organizations paralyzed and incapable of turning disruption into opportunity.

Leadership doesn't fit into straight lines and simple templates. It's complicated and sometimes messy, and blind spots abound. Herd mentality and the curse of sameness are two of the most prominent leadership blind spots, and nobody wants to fail. Still, the new operating reality demands a radically different approach to leadership, where disruption is the norm and not taking a risk is a risk. Every leader loves the "shiny new thing," and AI is a shiny new thing on steroids. However, the curse of sameness worries me because the future is more than technology or Gartner's latest tech hype cycle.[38] Our leadership models, beliefs, and assumptions about the future need a major overhaul. Leading and thriving in the unknown and turning volatility into upside requires iterative mindsets over fixed ones and acceptance that our leadership mindsets and behaviors need an upgrade.

The future is still being written, which excites me and gives me hope. It's a call to humility and a call to boldness. Despite accelerating business disruption and change powered by an AI and Geopolitical Supercycle, leadership will decide the future. My sense of urgency for *The Upside of Disruption* grew from these roots because risk and reward always travel in the same elevator, and standing still is akin to moving backward. Tennis legend Billie Jean King (BJK) said, "Pressure is a privilege." Leadership is a privilege, too. It's time to rip up the rulebook for leadership and make disruption a tailwind for better leaders, humane technology, and bolder futures.

- It's about the **curiosity** to close the gap between what we know and must know to lean into the future and turn it into a "challenge and grow" rather than taking a "wait and see" approach.

- It's the **courage** to unlearn the always-done ways and taken-for-granted norms about what leadership is, what it isn't, and how leaders can evolve to seize the future boldly.

- The **clarity** to separate headline risks above the noise and sharpen priorities is crucial when cultures of distraction, overload, and technology make the new but trivial seem urgent.

- The **collective trust** to win together, knowing that the thousands of daily decisions and choices matter, and elevate trust and purpose in each other, especially during extreme pressure.

New realities demand new thinking, difficult choices, and conversations about what stays, what changes, and what goes in the future of leadership. For instance, emerging trends and signals are significant forces that shape the world and disrupt the business landscape but also, more immediately, can unlock enormous growth opportunities and give leaders a unique chance to reimagine a bolder future. AI will be a megatrend radically transforming how we connect, create, lead, and work. Yet, many organizations still view it as a way to drive efficiency and lower costs through automation rather than a pivotal moment to rethink what it means to be a more humane organization. How can leaders harness AI's full potential to scale a future that maximizes human and business vitality? It starts with finding the upside in disruption.

UPSIDE OF DISRUPTION

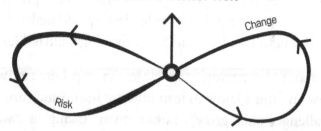

The Nutritional Value of Leadership

Not long ago, I attended a talk by English designer Thomas Heatherwick to discuss his new book, *Humanise: A Maker's Guide to Building Our World.* Heatherwick's studio is dedicated "to making the physical world around us better for everyone." Some of Heatherwick's most famous designs include the "Vessel," a futuristic staircase, and the "Little Island," a place to escape from Manhattan. Next time you're in New York, they are must-see designs. Heatherwick's book is a manifesto for courage, exploring how buildings and cities everywhere have lost their soul and what we can do about it. It's true. Most buildings are the worst places to be creative. Worse, their boring designs, low ceilings, inadequate ventilation, and sleep-inducing décor make us feel tired and depressed. The best ideas rarely come from inside the office. As entrepreneur and educator Steve Blank says: "Get out of the building,"[39] which refers to getting to know our customers and understanding their pain points, the source code of all game-changing inventions. As Heatherwick made a passionate case for humanizing our buildings and starting a national conversation about it, it occurred to me that we should also be having a national conversation about humanizing our leadership because, despite this age of disruptive AI and algorithms, leaders must still operate at the human scale: connection, belonging, and trust.

Is your leadership style best described as a "preserver" or "challenger" of the status quo? One of the blind spots leaders must overcome to seize the upside of disruption is not being trained in leadership. It's seen as more of an art and instinct than a repeatable set of mindsets, skills, and practices. That's a problem because it leaves employees stuck in conformity behaviors; we're not trained in courage and human skills (seeing, feeling, being, and listening to learn). We're only trained in "knowing." Leaders can't be what they can't see. They must be alert to the curse of sameness when it happens and explore the contrarian view because that's where the upside of disruption is found.

Hack Future Lab's research shows that a third of employees strongly agree that "their voice doesn't matter at work," and a quarter report going to work "feeling anxious or scared." Most teams feel powerless during periods of extreme volatility, and many leaders are lost in echo chambers and feel overwhelmed by the pace of change.[40] Look at the flurry of recent firms that, without warning, fire their employees in one-way video call announcements and statements such as "If you're on this call, you are part of the unlucky group being laid off."[41] Heatherwick observed, "Do our buildings give us nutritional value and leave us feeling more alive and empowered?" The question for leaders is, "Does our leadership deliver nutritional value through how we honor the past, define the present, and champion the future?" Or, "Does our leadership make others feel powerless and scared of leaning into the future?" Leadership is on the ballot. Today's difficult-to-predict challenges can't be solved with traditional leadership models.

The *Upside of Disruption* is a radically human approach to eliminating outdated mindsets and assumptions about the basic building blocks of leadership – data, agility, risk, and evolution– and answers the question, "Do we continue to lead with Industrial Age mindsets or adapt to the Intelligence Age?" Future readiness is the ability to empower, adapt, and thrive despite uncertainty. In the twentieth century, processes ruled organizations, and economist Frederik Taylor declared that "the system must come before the person." Now, mindsets drive the processes, and competition is no longer just companies versus companies. It's about mindsets versus mindsets.

This upending of taken-for-granted norms in Data, Agility, Risk, and Evolution – **DARE** – offers leaders at every level in an organization a new leadership blueprint to win in the

Intelligence Age, chart a new course to the future, and say goodbye to the status quo.

- **Data: Lead with AI**

  The leadership team of a 50,000-plus organization sent a personalized "thank you" message to every individual worldwide using their first name and local language. AI made creating and editing these messages much easier and quicker than usual, compressing the cost and time it would take from weeks to minutes. The stunt was intended to highlight the need to lead with AI because no vertical will be left unaffected by AI-driven disruption, and those firms that renew their lease on the future will be the ones that can turn tectonic changes into learning and growth. Over the last three years, one truth has emerged with undeniable clarity: All firms are now AI-centric. AI will change the nature of everything, but the story of AI is still being written. AI is sucking up electricity, cash, copyrighted data, and even water. It's not sustainable. What are the promises and perils of AI, and will it be an enabler or a threat that risks putting entire professions out of a job? Will the future be automated or augmented, or will a dystopian AI golem mine us of our humanity? Imagine this scenario. Rather than paying hundreds of thousands of dollars for consultants to recommend a new growth strategy, a CEO could ask an AI Co-Strategist for the three best strategic options and select the best.

  AI will add further complexity to culture and leadership as humans evolve from Homo Sapiens to Techno Sapiens, living and working alongside AI as co-creators. In the Era of Co-Intelligence, the upside is not a given, and risks are the norm. On the one hand, technology has the potential to automate the boring parts of our jobs and free up time to deliver more meaningful and higher-value work. Still, it also leads to record levels of automation anxiety about the future, with two-thirds of people strongly agreeing that "I worry about losing my job to AI in the next five years."[42] Anxiety and a lack of optimism about the future are like oil and water. They are trust destroyers.

Leading with AI means that every leader is now in a tech firm operating at light speed. Still, you will need human maximization to stand out in a sea of sameness: a return on imagination and the courage skills of contrarianism, proactive resilience, and risk-taking. The difference will be human ingenuity over what historian Yuval Harari calls "artificial intimacy" or, worse, "artificial idiocy."[43] Leadership will become increasingly decentralized, dispersed, and algorithmically driven. The leaders who unlock the vast untapped potential of their talent will allocate more time and resources to frontier leadership: a mindset of improvising, adapting, and harnessing AI not just as another tool but as a platform for innovation and reinvention. Leading with AI is more than a new chapter for leaders to navigate. It's an entirely new story, and there's no one-size-fits-all strategy.

- **Agility: Great leaders unlearn**

Are you a complexifier or a simplifier? Every organization aspires to be agile, and the word "agility" is mentioned thousands of times a day in meetings, earning calls, and board rooms. Yet, there's a big gap between rhetoric and reality. Most organizations are too slow, siloed, and complicated. Hack Future Lab's findings reveal that while most organizations recognize agility as a top strategic priority, only 15% describe themselves as having widespread agile behaviors. The agility paradox highlights the crucial role of unlearning because when you leave something behind you gain something too.[44] When leaders fail to unlearn the always-done ways, they become overwhelmed with obsolete working and leadership styles that slow decision-making and erode value. They should let go of outdated "best practices" that no longer serve their purpose and are now considered "broken practices."

The fictional coach Ted Lasso said, "Stay teachable." Unlearning is the ultimate form of proactive resilience to adapt, diversify, and stay ahead of disruption in the Intelligence Age. In the twentieth century, organizations focused on control, efficiency, and economies of scale. Today, in a post-industrial world, the focus is on economies of learning, ecosystems of trust, and social capital. However, access to social capital has gone way down, with fewer than 15% of US workers reporting that their network has grown in the last year.[45] That's a problem because social capital increases resilience and creativity as ideas travel faster through networks than hierarchies. In a rapidly changing environment where company life spans are shortening, leaders should constantly build social capital and embrace diverse perspectives. For example, one pharma client I'm advising (let's call it Prometheus) has introduced an enterprise-wide platform of unlearning that empowers more than 115,000 people to unlearn working practices and inefficient meetings that stop employees from doing their best work. We are all responsible for unlearning. "The key is agility, agility, agility," as Microsoft's CEO, Satya Nadella, says.[46]

Mindsets of collective action are essential to agility-led cultures. Most leaders focus too heavily on nitpicking, efficiency, and protecting past legacy rather than rethinking the purpose of an organization.

Norges Bank Investment Management (NBIM) manages Norway's $1.5 trillion sovereign wealth fund and has put rethinking cycles at the center of its leadership. Anthropologists have been invited to visit the firm to understand the forces driving its culture and strategy. The CEO of NBIM, Nicola Tangen, says, "The thinking was: if it's good, then it is good. If it's bad, it is good because then we know what to improve!"[47] Reimagining how leadership gets done is a crucial question for those who want to avoid getting sidetracked by over-confidence cycles: humility over hubris is one of the best ways to stay relevant in an era of perpetual beta and remain agile and future-ready.

- **Risk: The courage advantage**

  Multiplying and overlapping trends, from unprecedented AI-driven disruption and lower transaction costs to demographic shifts and connectivity, are poised to unwind the old leadership rules. Now, we have cross-industry competition and sectors colliding, where your next biggest competitor could come from an adjacent industry. The courage advantage is essential to leading the future and pushes leaders to sharpen their growth and value agendas and question what's changing in their business. As the rate of change accelerates, so must the rate of courage, driving the business outside its comfort zone.

  Today, leaders must make things happen with flexibility and skill to pivot as market conditions change and need boldness in three areas: Who we are, how we operate, and how we grow. Take the story of Stora Enso, a Finnish pulp and paper manufacturing firm whose history dates back more than seven hundred years. Firms must be prepared to do things differently as the world changes faster. The worldwide decline in paper demand severely impacted Stora Enso's bottom line, forcing the leadership team to look hard in the mirror and ask, "Why?" For Stora Enso's leaders, it meant acknowledging that their mindsets and assumptions were no longer viable for a fast-changing world and that industry disruption was an opportunity to adapt. They understood that the era of prioritizing profit above all else was ending. Instead, they showed the foresight to embrace their billion-dollar beliefs, such as digitalization, sustainability, and decarbonization. Can courage be a strategic advantage? Stora Enso has answered the question by pivoting faster than its peers toward the future. They have invested their billion-dollar beliefs into the global transition to renewable energy and become a significant player in the global bioeconomy. Stora Enso has defined its future growth story with daring and tenacity.[48]

Humans are sometimes irrational and unpredictable, which can give credence to the idea that anything is possible. A healthier and more sustainable approach is to harness the courage advantage. Nearly 73% of CEOs and CFOs list courage among the top three factors driving long-term financial performance. Hack Future Lab's research on firms with the courage advantage found that their returns to shareholders outperformed their peers by 18% over five years.[49] The courage advantage is the capacity to play offense and defense and leverage disruption as a call to mobilization. One mindset is daring to unlock the upside in disruption, launching new products, services, and business models. The other mindset is prudence in managing the downside, being at the top of your peer group for talent, efficiency, and productivity. Meta's stock has gained more than 178% in the last year despite strategic missteps, including losses of more than $100 billion on the metaverse.[50] When volatility is high, being 10% more proactive or 10% bolder is an edge and a powerful way of turning adversity into advantage.

- **Evolution: In trust, we grow**

Money is the currency of transactions, and trust is the currency of future readiness. As the automation of jobs threatens to undermine trust in our leadership and organizations struggle to retain top talent, trust-focused leadership is a source of resilience and future growth. According to Hack Future Lab, 67% of people do not believe today's organizations are fit for purpose, and one-third of people think their jobs will not exist in a few years due to AI and automation.[51] The politics of deglobalization and global labor supply problems favor ChatGPT, Gemini, and the strategy of "AI everywhere" and can undermine trust in organizations. Transformations don't fail because of technology. They fail because of a lack of trust.

Trust is on the ballot, too. More firms are operating at the edge of trust, and the commercial and human implications are significant, with the impact on businesses alone estimated to cost organizations more than $7 trillion globally in lost productivity. According to Hack Future Lab's Trust Decay study, ten out of fifteen industry sectors have reported a collapse in trust over the last three years, and plenty of examples explain why.[52] WeWork's rise to $47 billion darling of Silicon Valley, with its vision of transforming the future of work into a tech-enabled lifestyle and its subsequent dramatic fall to bankruptcy, offers leaders a valuable lesson in the risks of short-sighted financial engineering and a hype-fueled strategy that eroded trust in the leadership. Another example is Silicon Valley Bank's (SVB) $20 billion collapse, which stemmed from risky practices and lack of board oversight and scrutiny, while regulators also missed red flags. Multiple scandals damaged trust in the bank, and inadequate governance left SVB acutely vulnerable from overexposure to risky investments and insufficient cash reserves as interest rates rose.[53]

As the demise of WeWork and SVB shows, an exchange of trust defines every leadership action and decision, and yet, at no time has trust been more tested or valued by each other. Within every organization, leaders face a simple question: How do we get the best from our people? Trust is the answer. Trust is a leap of faith into the future and is a hallmark of helping others find the upside in disruption. This provides a helpful starting point for rethinking our leadership trust and shines a spotlight on what the future might hold, for better or worse.

The DARE framework sharpens two vastly underutilized mindsets, agility and courage, and is the foundation of finding the upside in disruption. With the DARE framework, leaders at any level can learn to embrace evolution in all areas of their business: mindset, culture, talent, and strategy.

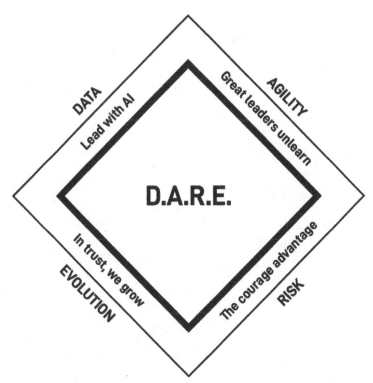

In each chapter, I explore how leaders can use the DARE framework to differentiate themselves and reimagine a bold, resilient future. The stakes couldn't be higher, and the opportunity couldn't be more significant. Most business books are like a sugar rush without nutrition. I hope *The Upside of Disruption* is different. I want to give leaders a wake-up call from the future because we always overestimate the risk of trying something new and underestimate the risk of staying still. What follows are the stories of leaders and their organizations who have found the upside in disruption. When the world changes, we must dare to evolve and be ready to get started. This book will be your guide.

Data: Lead with AI

"Software is eating the world, but AI is going to eat software."
– Jensen Huang, CEO of NVIDIA

*B*lack Mirror is a Netflix series about the dark side of technology set in a not-so-distant dystopian future. In each episode, unsettling stories unfold of how science and technology collide with humanity in unexpected and terrifying ways. If you're a fan of *The Twilight Zone*, you should watch *Black Mirror*. In one episode, "The Entire History of You," everyone has access to a memory implant the size of a grain called "Grain Technology" that records everything they see, hear, and do. People can re-watch and edit all their memories with devastating consequences for their mental and emotional well-being. What seems like a technology that initially empowers society inadvertently leads to paranoia, jealousy, and despair because people cannot forget or "let go."[1]

I've had my own *Black Mirror* moment. I received an email from Amy Ingram, who contacted me on behalf of her CEO to set up a meeting in New York. Nothing was strange about that, but when I met with the CEO later that week, he asked me, "What did I think of Amy's emails?" I replied that I thought it was an unusual question; however, Amy's emails were "fine," and she was "fast and responsive" during our email exchange. The CEO smiled, paused, and looked at me. "I have a confession," he said. Amy isn't "human"; she's AI, and the clue is in her initials, Amy Ingram (AI). My first reaction was embarrassment. I had been chatting with Amy and even asked how her day was going, to which she replied, "Really well, thanks." My subsequent reaction was paranoia. Had I unwittingly become part of a *Black Mirror* episode?

My final reaction was awe. Cars that can drive themselves, platforms that can anticipate our every need, and robots capable of everything from advanced manufacturing to complex surgery. This is not the age of disruption. It's the Age of Wonder, what science fiction writer Arthur C. Clarke called "any sufficiently advanced technology is indistinguishable from magic." I could barely sleep that night. To observe Amy Ingram mimic an incredibly humanlike conversation in a few seconds, I realized that science fiction has become a science fact: AI will change everything about how we do everything, including how we lead, how we work, how we create, and how we compete. It's leading with AI. The waves of disruptions we see today, which we assume are moving fast, are likely only the start because AI is the first tool in history that can:

1. Create new things by itself

2. Make decisions by itself

When I was at college, software came in a box. Later it came "as a service," and today you can create software using AI. AI will upend our assumptions about intelligence and productivity, creating a multiplier effect as the time to complete tasks collapses, but it's more than hyper-efficiency. For instance, the curve is almost tilted straight up if you consider the productivity journey from railroads to AI (measured by GDP per hour worked). As AI researcher Geoffrey Hinton says, "Generative AI is not just a faster way to find or assemble information." It will herald a new intelligence era where employees have human superpowers.[2] How will leaders harness all this intelligence and productivity to operate as a profitable organization that potentially creates existential risks (e.g., computers outsmart humans) and concentrates power in a way that increases biases and inequalities? Will humans be redundant or renewed? And will AI be as consequential as fire or electricity, or will AI, like crypto, be completely overhyped? The media loves to catastrophize about AI, but relative to the upside, the risks may be greater with gambling, for example.

AI Future Readiness

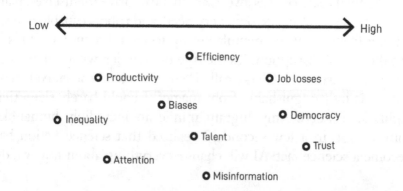

Low ←————————————————————→ High

- Efficiency
- Productivity
- Job losses
- Biases
- Inequality
- Democracy
- Talent
- Trust
- Attention
- Misinformation

Leadership Disrupted

Change used to happen as a breeze. Now, it feels like a category-5 typhoon. A Tech Supercycle is under way, with a staggering investment in dollars, data, and processing power. AI is converging and multiplying in ways that will transform the global economy, scaling equity market capitalizations potentially to $200 trillion by 2035.[3] If the war in Ukraine placed a spotlight on energy security and decarbonization, the pandemic accelerated digitalization and AI. AI adoption by companies over the next 10 years will continue to grow exponentially, creating tremendous upside as newcomers leverage hyper-automation, decentralized leadership, and AI to boost profitability and deliver more business value. To put that into perspective, digital e-commerce giant Shein would now be worth the same as SpaceX, H&M, and Zara if these were combined.

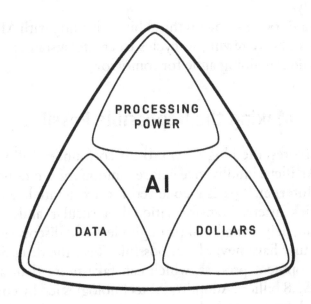

This is the new leadership logic: algorithms as a labor force and a winner-take-all effect. Welcome to leading in the "New

Meta," which is like changing the rules of chess halfway through a game. It's no longer organizations versus organizations: It's return on intelligence because AI radically lowers an organization's cost base while augmenting human capability to address its most urgent and immediate business priorities, such as tackling low productivity. Imagine spending 30% of your week doing tick-boxing tasks with little or no value. This is the sobering reality for many of us. With AI as a co-thinker, it's possible to automate low-value, routine tasks and reclaim more time to focus on problem-solving, strategic thinking, and high-growth initiatives that MIT researcher Cal Newport calls "Deep Work" rather than "Shallow Work."[4] The challenge for leaders is that you can't scale an exponential human-led, AI-enabled future with linear thinking. Consider this scenario: If up to 30% of hours worked by employees today could be automated by 2030 with the adoption of AI, leaders must think differently.

Like a Phoenix – the mythical bird – leading with AI is about rethinking and renewing in cycles to create sustained value for today while remaining agile for tomorrow.

Making the Impossible Possible

In GatesNotes, the blog of Microsoft co-founder Bill Gates, he writes: "Artificial intelligence is as revolutionary as mobile phones and the Internet."[5] AI is a code red for accelerated reinvention because it's utterly transformational, a secular and structural megatrend, delivering breakthrough ideas and discoveries across domains that have never been possible. Take the drug discovery and development process, which can take more than a decade and cost $2.8 billion. Adopting AI technologies led by companies such as AI-first biotech Insilico Medicine can yield "time and cost savings of at least 25–50%" in drug discovery up to the pre-clinical stage.[6] This Cambrian Explosion is driven by visionary capital, staggering processing power, computer chips, and large language models (LLMs).

The Cambrian Explosion refers to how life grew exponentially 500 million years ago and changed everything. We know the vital Cambrian eras of the last 500 years: Gutenberg's printing press, the scientific and medical revolution, the industrial revolution, the mobile and internet revolution, and now this moment. Frontier technologies such as AI require "frontier leaders" who can adapt, improvise, and overcome obstacles, taking concrete steps to adopt and operationalize AI while managing its associated risk.[7]

Disruption starts at the edges and speeds up, impacting organizations on both the supply and demand sides. AI can replace large parts of an organization by digitizing and automating processes and tasks and re-platforming to the cloud. Companies are sitting on a goldmine of diverse data that is becoming more significant daily. AI will enable these organizations to move from spreadsheets to self-service analytics and data silos to speed-to-learning, ultimately reducing the time to prepare analyses and make decisions. Palantir Technologies is a data analytics pioneer whose early years focused on detecting fraud but has since moved into military intelligence and healthcare. Now, it is betting big on AI to escape macroeconomic headwinds. With its staggering leadership in AI and data analytics, there's no reason why it could not disrupt the $700 billion global accounting industry.[8] At the same time, text-to-video like OpenAI's *Sora* film generator could be the next Hollywood disruptor. Leaders can't assume business as usual anymore.

Disruptive forces akin to the "Amazonification" of the global economy become the norm, leading to the rapid shrinking of companies, products, or job life spans and the need to embrace evolution continuously. Industry disruption is universal; any firm can drop from hero to zero regardless of market share and scale. The new reality means that leaders are now competing on Amazonification principles. Like the perennial disrupter Amazon, leaders must learn at the speed of the customer, crush bureaucracy, and embrace what Austrian economist Joseph Schumpeter called "the gales of creative destruction."

Amazonification Principles

- Economies of scale to *economies of learning*
- Supply chains to *AI-driven supply brains*
- Vertical power to *horizontal trust*
- Growth at any cost to *humanity and ecology*
- Fragmented control to *networked resilience*
- Cultures of conformity to *cultures of curiosity*

Imagine if Apple used its software muscle to disrupt the $2.86 trillion automotive industry or ChatGPT-search upends Google's multi-billion-dollar search business.[9] Now, the disruptors are even being disrupted. Everything the internet did to music and newspapers now happens to every other industry. We're operating in a world of venture-backed unicorns and decacorns like ByteDance's TikTok and Stripe, transforming markets as varied as EV cars, fintech, and healthcare.

To lead with AI, every leader must pay attention to the baseline fallacy, which is the assumption that the current leadership or business model is a low-risk bet until it isn't, at which time it is too late to do anything. Remember when Netflix shares fell more than 70%, wiping billions off its market cap?[11] Longer-term sustained success becomes harder and rarer, and the risk of organizations being derailed by the baseline fallacy increases as disruption grows. Whether it's the platformization of consumer financial services or the rise of the Algorithmic Society, the disruptive trends driven by AI will only multiply.

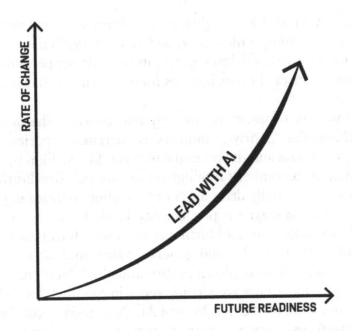

Leaders should always be cautious of hype cycles. Remember the Metaverse, Web 3.0, and NFTs? Contrast that to smartphones, e-commerce, and the race to the cloud, which have had much more lasting impacts on investment, the labor market, and the broader economy. How do we capitalize on these emerging disruptive forces and shape the future with bold intentionality?

The Most Significant Risk Is Not AI

AI-driven disruption itself is not the biggest threat to an organization's existence. The biggest threat is what the late management thinker Peter Drucker called "acting with yesterday's logic" and leaders becoming prisoners of the mental models of their past and current successes.[11] Amara's Law states that we tend to overestimate the effect of technology in the short run and underestimate its impact in the long run. Leaders must embrace Amara's Law to thrive in a "Forever Beta" world of perpetual learning, unlearning, and relearning. What happens when we remove historical constraints on scale, scope, and speed that have restricted organizations for 175 years? It has limitless potential.[12]

Viewed as a frontier technology that reshapes the future of everything, the AI-driven industry is currently experiencing a 43% growth rate and the potential to reach $1.5 trillion by 2030, according to Bloomberg Intelligence estimates.[13] Breakthroughs in AI can "potentially drive a 7% or $7 trillion increase in global GDP and raise stagnant productivity levels by 1.5% over ten years," according to Goldman Sachs. The McKinsey Global Institute finds that AI could generate value equivalent to $2.6 trillion to $4 trillion in global profits annually.[14] New entrants to the burgeoning sector are already receiving multi-billion-dollar valuations. One of them is Mistral AI, the one-year-old French AI start-up that creates humanlike text, media, and code within seconds. Leading with AI requires mental bifurcation: a dual mindset of boldness in exploring the upsides of AI and prudence in managing the downsides.

Underhyped Versus Overhyped

Will AI be the most disruptive force in history? Embracing AI is not just an option – it's a leadership priority. AI could solve the energy crisis, add trillions to the global economy, or wipe out the human race. When grasping how AI could reshape business, consider the other significant innovation of our time: GLP-1 medications like Ozempic and Wegovy. Both aid in weight loss by suppressing cravings. AI could become the equivalent of a corporate Ozempic encouraging CEOs to shed excess weight in their firms and make record layoffs. As Scott Galloway, Professor of Marketing at NYU Stern School of Business, writes in his blog *No Malice/No Mercy*: "Similarly, my thesis is that firms (notably tech companies) have also discovered a weight loss drug and are also being coy about it. Recent financial news features two stories: layoffs and record profits. These are related. There's no mystery to the surface narrative. A company lays off 5%, 10%, or even 25% of its workforce, and, 6 to 12 months later, after severance pay and expenses are flushed through the P/L, its operating margin hits new heights."[15] Perhaps AI is already playing a larger role in layoffs than CEOs are willing to admit.

AI's future is more than a new challenge for leaders to overcome. Leaders are on the brink of a tech revolution that could spur hyper-innovation and growth but also deepen inequality, lower labor demand, and reduce hiring as AI applications execute many tasks currently performed by humans. A client I worked with (let's call it Myriad) reduced its reporting from an average of two days to 30 minutes, translating into 87% savings in time and effort and more time for intelligent work. The IMF's latest research warns that up to "40% of jobs will be impacted by AI and about 60% of employment in advanced economies."[16] According to the WEF, "half the global labor force will need reskilling by 2025."[17] An inclusive, human-led, AI-enabled future is not guaranteed, and leaders must keep an eye on the future, especially regarding skills diversification.

Steve Jobs, the visionary behind Apple, championed the idea of skills diversification. Speaking at a Stanford graduation, he shared how he ended up in a Japanese calligraphy class after leaving college early. At first, "none of this had even a hope of any practical application" and was unrelated to the field of computer science, where Jobs later made his mark. However, when Jobs founded Apple, Jobs combined his artistic skills with technology to reshape the digital world. "You can't connect the dots looking forward; you can only connect them looking backward," he observed, urging students to create disconnected "dots" and then "trust these will somehow connect in your future."[18] Leaders should do the same to find the upside of AI, unpacking skills diversification and "cognitive flexibility," to cite Rand Spiro, a professor of educational psychology at Michigan State University, to prepare their organizations for a Reskilling Revolution impacting more than 1 billion humans.[19]

A Brief History of AI

Writer William Gibson said, "The future is already here – it's just not evenly distributed."[20] The recent history of AI is unevenly distributed and can be broken down into multiplying and overlapping waves called the "3 E's."

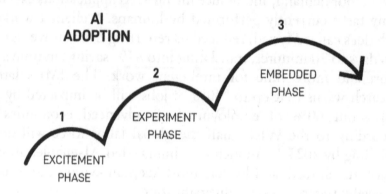

AI
ADOPTION

3

2   EMBEDDED
                     PHASE

1   EXPERIMENT
       PHASE

EXCITEMENT
PHASE

The first wave of AI was the "Excitement" phase, although the idea of AI and automation is not new. It goes back more than 2,000 years to Talos, the mythical bronze automation on the island of Crete. During the nineteenth century, mathematicians Ada Lovelace and Charles Babbage proposed the Analytical Machine, a mechanical general-purpose computer.[21] In the 1950s, MIT's Marvin Minsky, "the father of AI," helped create the vision for AI today with the Society of Mind Theory. The exponential acceleration of cost reductions, processing power, and network effects have only lately converged to make human work augmented with AI a reality. It took the cellphone 16 years to reach 100 million users, and it took OpenAI's ChatGPT just two months and appeared to reach its zenith when OpenAI was valued at more than $86 billion, which is the same as 40-year-old Dell Computers and 97-year-old Mercedes Benz.[22] Every CEO extolled the benefits of AI in earnings calls and how they plan to use AI to enhance products and services and capitalize on the productivity boom.

Founded as an academic discipline in 1955, AI is practically as old as the first digital computer. As with most emerging technologies, a gradual (though anything but smooth) convergence of performance improvements and cost reductions has only recently conspired to make AI a boardroom-relevant agenda item. In the Intelligence Age, AI is more than a faster way to find information. It will unlock collective intelligence and speed to creativity across the organization, creating synergies and diverse perspectives developed through the cross-pollination of ideas. The hope is that AI will supercharge not just profit maximization but human maximization, but risks and concerns remain high.

Alphabet has led the Excitement phase with the highest number of AI mentions, with CEO Sundar Pichai mentioning "AI" 64 times in one earnings call and proclaiming it has embedded "deep computer science and AI" in all its product updates.[23] Yet, knowing that another nascent technology called the Metaverse was on every CEO's lips not long ago is worth remembering. Today mentions of it in earnings calls have dropped nearly 50%, according to estimates by Hack Future Lab, and media and entertainment giant Disney, Inc., has shut down its Metaverse department with more than 50 employees as part of a cost-cutting program.[24] The shiny new thing can easily blind business leaders: AI has yet to impact most companies. According to the Pew Research Center, about 6 in 10 US adults (58%) are familiar with ChatGPT, though relatively few have tried it themselves.[25]

During AI's excitement phase, leaders must "start before they're ready," exploring and working with AI with a spirit of openness and curiosity and sharing insights and experiences (the good, bad, and ugly) with others across the business. This is the best way to demystify and humanize AI and understand its potential significance and limitations.

The second wave of AI is the "Experimentation" phase. According to Goldman Sachs, investment in AI technologies could increase 4X to $200 billion by 2025, and Generative AI firms make up 60 percent of new unicorns valued at $1 billion or more.[26] AI is the "internet" moment of our time and the top investment priority for leaders after innovation and talent. Leaders in the experimentation phase of AI are testing Generative AI sandboxes, using AI as a co-thinker to support problem-solving and collaboration, and building their AI use cases across different functions to reinvent the customer experience, enhance productivity, and realize the business value of AI. Hack Future Lab's research estimates productivity gains of up to 40% for employees who use AI compared with those who don't. This requires a significant shift in mindsets, cultures, and capabilities for a post-AI world, and this is arguably where the most prominent innovations will be. Hack Future Lab's research shows that frontier leaders demonstrate a high learning orientation when leading with AI, starting with framing a narrative about humans and machines and asking practical, sense-making questions that ensure AI doesn't dehumanize leadership.[27]

- Will AI be the great equalizer? If not, why not?
- How do we internally communicate the promises and perils of AI to our employees, co-creating the future together?
- How do we align AI to serve the best interests of all our stakeholders?
- Will AI turbocharge profits at the expense of ethics?
- How do we ensure AI aligns with our vision and purpose for meaningful impact?
- How do we set ourselves up to scale ethical AI that's secure, trusted, and governed correctly?
- How do we select the tech and talent stack to support our AI-enabled journey?

- How do we manage AI concerns around data privacy, misinformation, and security?

- How do I work alongside AI to become a Super Leader?

- How can we harness AI confidently and responsibly while elevating what makes us more human?

Allocating accountability in the era of algorithmic decision-making can pose significant challenges. Asking questions about harnessing AI and involving your team in the exercise is a simple yet powerful way to consider the risks and challenges of becoming a "human-led, AI-enabled" organization. Questions help us think and listen, and listening creates transparency and trust, essential to reducing tech-induced anxiety (will AI displace me?) and re-focusing on empowering others. Trust is built through actions, not words, and movements such as "AI Needs You," a humanist manifesto for the age of AI by Verity Harding, formerly of Google DeepMind, and industry-wide initiatives like the #ChangeTheFace Alliance. #ChangeTheFace is a community of technology companies collaborating to make the tech industry more human-led and inclusive. The alliance has created a set of Post-AI Guiding Principles to make technology more humane.[28]

AI's third and final wave is the "Embedded Everywhere" phase. Social media wires the world for engagement and AI for intimacy. Industry convergence, cost constraints, and talent scarcity favor the rise of AI, and collaboration between humans and machines (cobots) will be the norm in most advanced economies by 2030. AI may have surpassed human intelligence, becoming so ubiquitous and embedded in business and society that it's "invisible," according to some futurists such as Ray Kurzweil, and most devices we use today, from appliances to toys, will be embedded with AI, anticipating our needs with predictive "all-knowing" algorithms.[29] AI's third wave will create a fully connected, intelligent world, with the volume of data worldwide growing more than 10 times to more than 600 zettabytes, equivalent to 610 iPhones (128GB) per person. That's more data than all the grains of sand on the planet.

As the future accelerates, AI will substantially transform every industry, and its impact on the future of leadership, trust, and strategy is unquestionable. A wait-and-see approach is a risky choice; it is far better to adopt a dare-and-explore one.

What will AI's black swan event be in the "Embedded Everywhere" phase? AI can potentially increase efficiency and innovation but also introduces certain systemic risks. We've already seen the dangers of placing too much trust in technology. Whether it's the British Post Office and Fujitsu Software Accounting Scandal or AI Bots cursing customers, leaders must replace hubris with humility to avoid being seduced by AI's dizzying acceleration.[30] Deepfakes and voice cloning will put cybercrime on steroids, reaching $10.5 trillion by 2025, and a major fiscal event becomes more likely thanks to more advanced algorithms, increased data volumes, and quantum processing power.[31] Balancing innovation with regulatory oversight is crucial for the long-term success of AI as regulators such as the US Securities Exchange Commission (SEC) raise concerns about data protection, antitrust, and market stability. *The New York Times* is suing OpenAI and Microsoft for copyright infringement, opening a new legal battleground over the unauthorized use of published content to train large language models (LLMs) and raising urgent questions about profits versus ethics.[32] We're at a regulatory tipping point. Ethical AI is a top leadership concern for embracing the "Embedded Everywhere" phase based on the need to regulate but not box companies in. It's leading with a human-led, ethics-first approach: Principles, Privacy, Accountability, Human-centricity, Transparency, and Security. Actively participating in co-developing new guardrails and regulations will be critical. For example, Inflection AI's founder, Mustafa Suleyman, calls for an International Panel on AI Safety to monitor and evaluate the progress of AI akin to the Intergovernmental Panel on Climate Change (IPCC).[33]

The story of AI is still unfolding, and leaders must think beyond the hype and hysteria of AI. Leaders all want to talk about AI, but they are not yet up to speed on what it is, what it isn't, and why it matters from an organizational perspective. Sensationalist headlines in the media are not helpful, although some are pretty funny. DPD, the global courier firm, had to turn off its artificial intelligence online chatbot after a customer could make the bot swear and write a poem criticizing the firm.[34] I came into contact with the hype about AI, too. I was invited to attend a Blockchain and AI Yoga event. I can't think of anything more terrifying than standing on my head while discussing the benefits of AI! But the most memorable story involves aircraft toilets. I attended a tech conference where one of the presenters spoke about airports planning to use AI to analyze wastewater samples when planes land at airports to scan for new viruses. Be careful next time you fly.

The AI-Intelligence Illusion

Not long ago, I visited the Netherlands and came across a grocery chain store called Jumbo, which dates back to the 1920s. Like most companies, Jumbo was no exception: The pandemic accelerated optimized reality, which includes e-commerce, digitalization, cost-cutting, and automation. Grocery chains have spent billions replacing humans with automated self-checkout machines, and today, according to Hack Future Lab's estimates, the number of self-checkout lanes in stores is 40%.[35] I walked around the store for 15 minutes and found a few items to take to the self-checkout, where I discovered a Kletskassa – the Dutch word for a "chat checkout." A chat checkout is like a slow lane for anyone who prefers human interaction over machines and is a welcome respite from the repetitive "unexpected items in the bagging area."

Chat checkouts are gaining support because we are suffering from a loneliness epidemic. US Surgeon General Vivek Murthy declared that an "epidemic of loneliness and isolation" was harming social and individual health. Today, 300 million people report having no friends, and 70% of seniors say they are "lonely" and "isolated."[36] The World Health Organization (WHO) has declared loneliness a global health risk, and the

Center for Humane Technology says it's a national security concern.[37] Perhaps not surprisingly, the chat checkout was the most popular lane at Jumbo with the longest queue. As I chatted with other people in the chat checkout, I concluded that "faster, cheaper, efficient" is not always a winning strategy and that trust in technologies such as AI to improve human lives is not a given. Today, Jumbo's chat checkout is its most profitable lane, and it plans to introduce more than 200 chat checkouts nationwide. This is the intelligence illusion whereby we place blind faith in technology to increase productivity and efficiency without understanding the impact on human behavior, culture, and trust.

Despite the rise of what Italian economist Mariana Mazzucato calls "consultification," the relentless pressure from external consultants to cut costs, and the hoped-for efficiency gains of automated self-checkouts, Jumbo has made the bold and counterintuitive decision to make human interaction a central part of its future growth strategy.[38] With loneliness rising and more than a billion people aged 65+ making up 20% of the global population, it's arguably a clever move for achieving long-term profitability and a primary reason why leaders should test their assumptions about technology and put humans first.[39] Understanding the differences between warm and cold tech is one of the best ways to avoid the AI intelligence illusion and catalyze a more humane future.

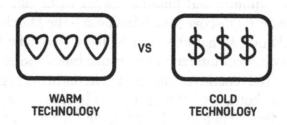

WARM
TECHNOLOGY

COLD
TECHNOLOGY

- **Warm tech** is a humanity-first future enabled by AI. It unlocks our full potential; increases trust, equity, and well-being; and elevates what makes us more human.

- **Cold tech** is a machine-first future powered by AI. It down-grades humanity, erodes trust, and amplifies hidden harms to our health and communities.

Warm Tech	Cold Tech
Reduces stress	Increases stress
Purpose and productivity	Bullshit jobs
Narrows equity gaps	Increases inequality
Treats attention as sacred	Makes the trivial seem urgent
Ethics over profits	Extractive business models
Strengthens communities and democracy	Drives addiction or loneliness
Empowers humans to flourish	Downgrades humans
Key Behavior Indicators (KBIs)	Key Performance Indicators (KPIs)

John Naisbitt was prescient in his prediction that "We are drowning in information but starved for knowledge."[40] While technology isn't the only reason, runaway AI is rapidly widening the intelligence gap further, leading to what's commonly known as the productivity paradox (also known as the Solow computer paradox). The productivity paradox is the surprising observation that as more investment is made in technology, employees' productivity may go down instead of up.[41]

Hack Future Labs research shows that:

- 73% of leaders agree they feel "overloaded and overwhelmed by the volume of daily emails"
- 69% of leaders report needing more daily time to do their jobs
- 56% of leaders report the rise of "ghosting" in organizations, whereby emails sent to others are ignored

- 53% of leaders agree that too much information hinders speed and agility
- 37% of leaders agree they spend too much time on transactional work over transformational

Source: Hack Future Lab

The emerging data is a warning signal that AI ironically may turbocharge the productivity paradox. We don't complete tasks faster because we use Excel spreadsheets, and the number of virtual and in-person meetings the average person attends daily has increased since the pandemic. Technology increases the expectation for leaders to "always be on," and doing more with less is a given. Messaging apps are a helpful reminder of the productivity paradox, too. Pitched as tools for businesses to connect people faster to the information they need, it quickly became apparent to many users that apps, social media, and now AI compete for our attention, effectively fooling us into thinking that something new but trivial is urgent. Productivity pressure is heating up, and "quiet" job cuts are rising. Will AI come to the rescue? The jury is still out on whether AI will finally solve the productivity paradox, but in the meantime, it's worth remembering that we're drowning in data and starved for information. Data isn't the new oil. Attention is the new oil.

Attention Is the New Oil

Leading with AI does not just mean faster; it means better and wiser: doing a few things and spending less time on changing policies and more on changing mindsets. Leaders are trustees of how time is spent, and attention is the rarest form of generosity a leader can give, yet we know it's not in good shape. A few months ago, I walked to a nearby pizzeria in downtown Manhattan to pick up a pizza. When I arrived, I collected the pizza and

returned to my hotel, looking forward to eating my fresh moz-
zarella pizza. I opened the pizza box and discovered no pizza
when I got to my room. Surprised, I walked back to the pizzeria
to explain what had happened. They had forgotten to put my
pizza in the box.

Hack Future Lab's research shows that focus and attention,
particularly leadership attention, has been downgraded, with
email and social media to blame:

- 84% of leaders agree that email and social media make the
  trivial seem urgent

- 77% of leaders agree that email and social media force us to
  multitask and over-commit

- 67% of leaders agree that email and social media weaponize
  FOMO (Fear of missing out)

Will AI serve humanity and be the ultimate intelligence multiplier? Writer Edward O. Wilson said, "We have Paleolithic
emotions, medieval institutions, and godlike technology. And it
is hazardous and approaching a point of crisis overall."[42] Our
evolved biology serves us well but also includes vulnerabilities
exploited by extractive attention business models and persuasive
technology (red dots, vibrations, and banners) that trigger our
salience network, fooling us into thinking everything is urgent.
Our emotional wiring and decaying institutions are dangerously
out of sync with the "godlike technology" that is AI, and we pay
a high price when our default leadership style is "rush and react"
rather than "think and decide."

There's less time to focus on "deep" leadership (connecting, listening, trusting, value-creating, and transformational
work), and too much time is wasted on shallow leadership
(autopilot, checking, bureaucracy, reacting, and transactional
work). So, how do you learn to lead with AI without overload
and burnout?

Here are five simple strategies why attention is the ultimate clarifier for leading with AI.

1. Focus on velocity, not speed

The reason is simple. Speed is the time rate at which we're moving along a path, while velocity is the rate and direction we're heading in. Speed without aligned direction can lead to strategy or culture drift and waste limited time and resources. As management thinker Morten Hansen says, "Do less, then obsess."[43]

2. Fight complexity with simplicity

When you encounter a problem you can't solve, don't make it smaller – make it bigger. Today's problems require new thinking, not old solutions. Thinking small and being an "incrementalist" depletes our boldness, essential to thriving in the age of AI. Embracing the urgency and scale of your biggest challenges will encourage you to evolve from linear thinking to exponential: divergent, creative, and daring.

3. Have meeting-free days and a "no" strategy

You're having too many meetings! Hack Future Lab's research highlights that the number of back-to-back meetings has doubled in the last two years and are often scheduled with no breaks in between. Too many wasteful meetings lead to a higher leadership tax (more time on bureaucratic work and less time to focus on higher-value work). Hack Future Lab's research shows that a meeting-free day can increase autonomy, focus, and execution speed by up to three times. Leaders are drowning in too many priorities and over-commitments. A "no" strategy is one of the best forms of optimization and a powerful way to protect focus and attention.

4. Fortify triple attention

Meta attention is paying attention to attention, and leadership attention is no different. This requires constant protection and investment to stay ahead of change and protect our future readiness and well-being. Leaders can fortify their attention by strengthening three different types of attention: Inner, Other, and Outer.

1. **Inner attention** focuses on gut-level intuition, reflection, and curiosity about learning and discovering new worlds and unexpected insights. It's about asking braver questions of ourselves and connecting deeply to our inner world where ideas and unspoken truths lie dormant. Making space to spark inner attention doesn't happen by accident. It takes an intentional and focused approach. Walking in nature and trying not to think too hard, almost like a brain break, helps me reconnect with my inner self.

2. **Other attention** focuses on others around you, building bridges, listening, collaborating, and growing together through human-to-human connection. It's generosity and reciprocity. With social health taking center stage and the loneliness epidemic declared a national emergency, other attention is a must-do priority. It's about rejecting artificial trust and how technology can sometimes diminish our humanity; for instance, the rise of "ghosting," where people ignore somebody rather than communicate with them. It is far better to put humans first, not technology.

3. **Outer attention** focuses on external trends and movements and staying alert to new signals and opportunities packaged as risk and reward. It's having an eye on the

future while making things happen today. For instance, once a month, a Future Friday event can inspire teams to step into the future and stretch their horizons beyond today to ask, "What's emerging?" and "What if?" Without collective attention on our outer world, it's easy to miss the wild card that could become the next game-changing product, service, or business model.

I hear that success breeds success, but success can also corrupt success and lead to so-called zombie leadership, with dead ideas and assumptions about work that refuse to die. Remaining ahead during constant disruption is difficult without committed and focused attention to our inner world (blind spots, reflection, well-being) and outer world (people, risks, change). Worse, leaders get trapped in their optimism bubbles and filter out bad news and helpful counterfactual thinking that can reduce risk or seize the upside. To paraphrase psychologist Daniel Kahneman, "We're blind to our blindness. We have very little idea of how little we know. We're not designed to."[44]

Leaders with heightened levels of inner and outer attention are significantly better at embracing humility to their faults and biases, recognizing hazards before they turn into crises, and finding new paths to agility. Leading with AI is not about speed itself. It's about deliberate and thoughtful attention to yourself, others, and the world around you. It's a shortcut to future readiness and trust in each other and a catalyst for human-centric leadership in a burnout world.

Matching AI with Leadership and Humanity

Behavioral scientist and author Rory Sutherland said, "The next revolution is not technological; it's psychological."[45] People want to thrive in agility-led cultures offering work that combines opportunity, growth, and skills over a lifetime and sustain what makes them more human: radiate meaning, belonging, and deep work that gives us dignity and pride. Data at the Mayo Clinic suggests that if less than 20% of our work consists of things we love to do, we are more likely to suffer from burnout (cognitive and emotional burnout) or "bore out" (e.g., emotional and cognitive underload). I'd argue leaders must aim higher than 20% and strive to build workplaces where most people love what they do.[46] It's time to question ways of leading that diminish what makes us human. A failure to reimagine how we work is a failure of leadership. Instead, avoid empty slogans and emphasize how humans and machines can co-exist in a way that gets the best from our talent, starting with the "Anything Workforce."

The Anything Workforce

Uncertainty is at peak levels when navigating the future of work, skills, and talent, not helped by leadership's short-termism and shareholder demands. Tomorrow's winners will make winning the skills revolution powered by AI a core part of their future readiness plan, like training their workforce for the Olympics without knowing which event they'll compete in. This is what Jeff Swartz, VP of Insights and Impact at Gloat, the AI-powered talent marketplace provider and the author of *Work Disrupted: Opportunity, Growth, and Opportunity in the Accelerated Future*, calls the "Anything Workforce" (agility, character, and cognitive skills), where work is value-focused, and career pathways are T-shaped. This is the opposite of the "One Thing" workforce (siloed, rigid, and fixed), where work is bureaucratic-focused, and career paths are I-shaped. Character and cognitive skills matter, too. Character skills, such as improvising, adapting, and overcoming problems, often indicate long-term impact over cognitive skills that are increasingly easy to automate or outsource to AI. As you decide about scaling AI in your organization, how you unbundle and re-bundle roles to strengthen character and cognitive skills will be a pivotal question for leaders.[47]

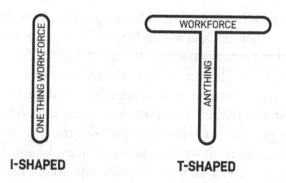

I-SHAPED   T-SHAPED

The future belongs to the "Anything Workforce" because our leadership challenges are more complex, interconnected, and urgent than ever, compounded by global talent scarcity. The London Interdisciplinary School (LIS) is unlocking the "Anything Workforce" through the power of cross-disciplinary thinking by breaking down artificial barriers to creativity and innovation. The goal is to equip students with iterative skill sets and mindsets to question, explore, and experiment so that they can embrace the diverse perspectives and hidden insights needed to rethink problems and find new solutions.[48] Emerging research at Hack Future Lab shows that a team of cross-disciplinarians will generate up to five times more innovative solutions together than siloed thinkers can do. When interdisciplinary themes instead of siloed ones are shared, a team's capacity to adapt and solve challenges increases by up to 4.7 X.[49] Tackling the world's biggest challenges will require bold ideas and ecosystems of trust and collective impact. Cross-disciplinary thinking is the answer and uncovers the hidden potential of "Ubuntu" – an African philosophy that "I thrive because we are." Ubuntu underscores the importance of cross-disciplinary impact and being better than the sum of our parts. The future of talent is not I-shaped (One Thing Workforce). It's T-shaped (The Anything Workforce).

Leadership is the ultimate source of momentum as leaders respond to remote and hybrid work models, humans and AI, internal mobility, and talent marketplaces. After rising on leaders' radars for the past few years, skills and talent are the best way to beat the forces of disruption and impact the bottom line. A talent marketplace harnesses AI to maximize internal mobility, growth, and choice. Organizations are restructuring into smaller, flatter entities, and traditional jobs and tasks are being unbundled into gigs, projects, and skills. Taking a "pixelated approach" to reimagining how work gets done means that much like graphics can be broken down into pixels, work can be broken down into smaller pieces, whether remote work, projects, or internal gigs.[50] My father worked in the same firm for 45 years and, in return, received generous benefits and a pension. He had one career; promotion was called the "career ladder." My career path is the opposite. I've worked in numerous industries, and my career ladder looks like a career climbing wall or squiggly line.

Today's flexible workforce means every job and project can be done by various people, each with a different preference for why, where, and how they work: remote and hybrid work, projects, tours of duty, and gigs. Yet, there's a significant aspiration-to-action gap in most organizations.

Hack Future Labs research shows that:

- 93% of leaders are worried about the impact of talent scarcity on growth plans
- 84% of leaders want to become skills-based organizations
- 49% of leaders don't have a race-to-reskill strategy in place
- 44% of leaders don't know what skills they have in their workforce
- 23% of leaders believe they can anticipate future-ready skills in their organizations

Source: Hack Future Lab

According to Hack Future Lab, the number one reason employees quit a job after money is a lack of internal growth opportunities, and most say that internal mobility is "not a strength" in their organizations.[51] The riskiest talent gaps aren't the ones we know about; they're bubbling under the surface. One of the most unmistakable signs of leading with AI is rethinking assumptions about identifying and retaining talent. As organizations pivot to the future, replacing silos with internal growth opportunities is a must-have imperative. Even job titles need reimagining as the forces of AI disrupt them, with recent examples such as Tech Philosopher, Distraction Prevention Coach (we could all go with one of those), and a "Director of Disruption" who confessed to me her job title was as popular as a funeral director.

To lead the future of work and talent, leaders should reject "present forward" thinking and taken-for-granted norms that extend existing assumptions to tomorrow. This leadership style of doing the same thing repeatedly may have worked well in a predictable world but is less relevant for leading in a complex and turbulent one. Instead, leaders should avoid zombie leadership (leading with dead norms and ideas from the twentieth century) and focus on future-readiness skills: connectivity, cocreation, and cognitive and character strengths. Companies such as Mastercard, Tata, and Epic Games champion this anti-zombie leadership principle by sharpening a dual purpose in their organizations. Dual purpose is a meaningful source of momentum for leading in times of uncertainty and complexity and can be broken down into two types:

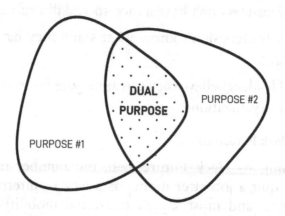

- **Purpose #1** is a significant organizational purpose that turns megatrends like sustainability or digitalization into practical milestones, with a narrative of making the future our business.
- **Purpose #2** is an individual leadership purpose, easily articulated and connected to knowing what you do makes a concrete difference and positively impacts others across the organization.

I met with the leadership team of a large pharma firm (let's call it Zenith) on a mission to sharpen its dual-purpose agenda. The meeting was held in Dubai, a city already living in the future where flying taxis and delivery drones will soon be a reality. Dubai even has its own Minister for AI. Zenith wanted to equip its workforce with the cognitive and character skills to thrive in sync with AI. The Chief Human Resources Officer (CHRO) said, "As the war for talent intensifies and working with AI increases, it has become more important than ever to put employees in the driver's seat of their careers. Internal surveys showed that nearly half of existing employees lacked internal mobility as their top reason for leaving the business. We had a reputation for being a 'frustration office' and 'damn bloody slow.' We prioritized increasing internal growth opportunities powered by AI, flexibility, and lifelong learning, called 'Future-fit.' Today, our workforce engagement scores are the highest they've ever been, and the word 'happy' is mentioned by our workforce. This never happened before."

With a fast-evolving global workforce of at least five different generations, the leadership team wanted to bring agility to placing the right talent in the right place at the right time. AI-powered talent marketplaces are a fast way to break down silos and match the supply and demand of talent within their organization and unleash the collective possibilities of their people. Dual purpose is the fuel that drives sustainable performance and can be sparked through matching talent to internal gig work, mentorships, projects, and career transitions that the talent marketplace provides. AI is the fuel to power it.

The challenges included:

- Prioritizing future readiness and agility
- Digital obsession and high learning orientation
- Deploying talent at scale to match business needs on demand
- Shift from "talent hoarding" to "talent sharing"
- Unlock hidden potential and productivity
- Leading with AI (fast, flat, human and hybrid)

The soft launch of the AI-powered talent marketplace at Zenith has seen more than 11,000 hours of productivity unlocked, $13.7 million in savings through internal mobility, and the most significant year-on-year increase in satisfaction for exceeding dual purpose within the organization. The firm is leading from the future in more agile ways, ultimately unlocking hidden potential and pushing others not to limit their challenges but to challenge their limits. Leaders must make game-changing moves to avoid becoming obsolete, learn new skills, and think in bold new ways to change the game. Since industry disruption is universal, every person must sharpen their future readiness edge: insights, trust, and execution. To paraphrase scientist Carl Sagan: "Extinction is the rule. Thriving is a choice."[52]

Be a Future-maker

Are you ready to lead with AI? The more digital we become, the more human we need to be. The reimagination of mindsets, culture, and capabilities in sync with the rise of AI may be the leadership imperative of the twenty-first century. We are at a watershed moment. Pessimists warn AI could wipe out humanity. Optimists hail a learning revolution. The most popular response is to assume that AI will vastly improve our lives, but what if the technology doesn't live up to its hype?

Will the future of AI be superhuman? Cultures of co-intelligence will help leaders be wiser and faster than the sum of their parts: speed to insight, speed to decision-making, and speed to execution. Yet, significant challenges remain in unlocking this superhuman power. Nothing can be taken for granted: Warm versus cold tech, efficiency versus empathy, and humans versus machines.

As Accenture CEO Julie Sweet says: "Most companies are not ready for AI rollout."[53] Data is at the heartbeat of future readiness, and most companies are still moving between the Excitement and Experimentation phases of AI as geopolitical risk and macro-uncertainty hold back investment. The question of our times will be for leaders to answer, "How do we align AI to serve humanity, empowering our teams with new superpowers?"

Takeaways

- **More human, less artificial:** If leaders consider the one thing they could do differently today to help people be more human in the age of AI, where would you start? A client I worked with (let's call them Delta Coffee) decided to introduce AI and machine learning into their coffee stores to analyze how productive the staff was, from receiving a coffee order to preparing and serving the coffee. Within a month of introducing AI, the speed of serving coffee had increased by 33%, but the team had not expected that the quality would go down. Worse, the motivation of the employees fell off a cliff because they felt they were working in a surveillance culture. Trust was severely damaged, and people's faith in AI as a tool for empowerment had been destroyed.

  To avoid alienation and your equivalent Delta Coffee's fate, take an intentional and human-centric approach: adopt a co-creation strategy to AI, take an iterative approach, and share stories and metrics that go beyond Key Performance

Indicators (KPIs) to evaluate objectively the hidden risks and unintended consequences of using AI. Instead, adopt Key Behavior Indicators (KBIs) that bring more humanity to leadership. Leaders must speak up about automation anxiety too, and show zero compromise on making AI ethical, fair, transparent, and safe. "Move slow and fix things" is a clarion call for leaders to be fully present, prioritize humans, and protect their most valuable asset: trust.

- **Rethink cultures:** Technological changes require cultural change, and we forget this principle at our peril. Most of us would agree that work has been "anti-agile" for too long: slow, siloed, and rigid. Leaders are under pressure from above and below, from silos and stress to skills gaps and slow decision-making. We're drowning in organizational stupidity that rewards bureaucratic work over intelligent work and doing things right *over* doing the right things. To unlock the full potential of AI, teams must be curiosity-driven. A culture of curiosity enables employees to explore the practical application of AI and is the secret to improving productivity and helping others thrive and lean into the unknown. Tech firm Airbnb has built a data and analytics culture by introducing a Data University to democratize AI skills and create a resilient, future-ready workforce. Employees feel energized and enabled to use AI as a co-pilot to do more value-creating work and waste less time on bureaucratic misery work. The future belongs to those who dare to learn and grow together. Now, employees have the right mindsets and skill sets across all functions to use AI tools and unlock their full potential, so leaders should not waste this reframing opportunity.[54]

- **Dare to evolve:** AI will redefine how and why we work, requiring leaders to co-create a compelling narrative about what AI is, what it isn't, and how to take concrete steps to experiment with it as a tool to make work more productive and meaningful. Build your AI use cases, test with co-pilots to "automate" the low-value task, and sharpen cross-disciplinary thinking. Leaders must also address urgent questions and concerns about automation, ethics, and job losses. I worked with a client who hosted a Future-Fit event once a month to tackle the most challenging questions about the future that kept everyone awake at night. Hack Future Lab's research shows that one-third of people are worried that "AI will take our jobs."[55] For some, AI still means the *Terminator* film starring Arnold Schwarzenegger or the specter of a "Hal" – the evil AI character in *2001: A Space Odyssey*.

If every firm is digitizing, only going deep sets you apart. Co-Intelligence means learning to thrive alongside AI with a beginner's mindset and a spirit of wonder. Leading with AI requires curiosity and courage. The curiosity to close the gap between what you know and want to know about AI and the courage to rethink assumptions about the purpose of leadership and the nature of work. As a leader, you can get overwhelmed by your inner doubts. Doubt becomes fear, and fear becomes the enemy of risk-taking. Starting before you're ready is the best way forward. The Japanese call the beginner's mindset *Shoshin*, the opposite of the expertise mindset. When the ratio of assumptions to knowledge is high, and there are many untested assumptions about AI, the best way to learn is to "do." A beginner's mindset of limitless possibility allows us to break out of the comfort zones of the Industrial Age and lean into the possibilities of the Intelligence Age.[56]

CHAPTER

3

Agility: Great Leaders Unlearn

"Half of wisdom is learning what to unlearn."

– **Larry Niven**

When was the last time you tried to unlearn something? In a recent fireside chat with Professor Amy Edmondson, the author of *The Right Side of Wrong: The Science of Failing Well*, we discussed why good leaders learn from mistakes, but the best leaders unlearn as well, whether it's outdated ways of working or taken-for-granted assumptions about leadership, or the future.[1] As a self-taught tennis player, I have experienced the personal challenge of unlearning how to serve a tennis ball. This was trickier than I expected, as I had to let go of the familiar and step into the unknown again. It required humility to recognize that I had terrible habits when I served and the vulnerability to speak to a coach to get help. When we watch professional tennis players compete, or any elite sports player, we think of their game as fully formed, but a player's game requires deliberate and focused unlearning, which I define as the capacity to reflect (Humility), rethink (Agility), and renew (Growth).

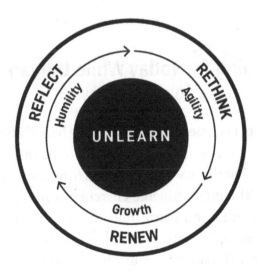

Unlearning could be the highest form of learning in a post-AI world. It's the ultimate insurance policy against zombie leadership (dead leadership that fails to adapt to changing circumstances) and "enshittification" – a term coined by academic Cary Doctorow to describe the slow decay in everything we do.[2] It is at the heart of every future-focused organization, allowing leaders to focus on accelerated growth and rethink outdated mindsets. At its core, unlearning is a leadership activity that helps us move from reactive to proactive resilience, tackling performance gaps *before* they occur; leaders update their assumptions and behaviors to make space for new learning and keep pace with change or even anticipate it. We can't put more into an empty cup. Unlearning ensures that busy, distracted leaders can overcome FOBO – Fear of Becoming Obsolete, stemming from blind spots such as narrow ambition (thinking too small), fragmented alignment (lack of unity), or execution certainty (lack of focus and commitment). Unlearning for leaders is a skill set but also a mindset for leaning into the discomfort of change and being willing to think and act differently to lead from the future, not the past.

Learning for Today While Unlearning for Tomorrow

Before futurists became a "thing," writer Alvin Toffler said, "The illiterate of the twenty-first century will not be those who cannot read and write, but those who cannot learn, unlearn, and relearn."[3] In leadership, the most valuable currency is not how much you know but how well you learn, relearn, and unlearn. Emerging research on neuroplasticity shows that our brains continuously create new growth pathways and discard others and that when we learn something new, we build new connections between our neurons. Like our leadership, our brains can adapt to new contexts, constraints, and challenges if we use unlearning to find the upside in disruption. The more I think about the limitless potential of unlearning, the more convinced I am that leaders share a universal shortcoming because there's a lot we need to unlearn as the world evolves faster and the "Half-Life of Everything" is speeding up the urgency to unlearn.[4]

The Half-Life of Everything is the time it takes for something to lose its currency before it is innovated away, and it's getting exponentially shorter as AI speeds up "disruption everywhere and all at once."

- The half-life of skills is 5 years, and technical skills are 2.5 years or less
- The half-life of competitive advantage is less than 18 months for S&P 500 companies
- The average CEO tenure of S&P 500 companies has decreased by 20% from 6 years in 2018 to 4.5 years today
- In science, the half-life of medical knowledge is 24 months, and it is projected to reach 100 days by 2027

Source: Hack Future Lab

As organizational speed increases, so must the rate of unlearning, or we risk falling behind and losing permanent relevancy. Disruption is the rule. The problem is that leaders need help to prepare for the Half-Life of Everything because they excel at adding complexity to complexity and have a bias against subtraction; they need to improve at elimination because they are drowning in data and information. Perhaps the challenge of our times isn't learning; it's unlearning.

It's time to unlearn old leadership mindsets, cultures, and accepted norms and say "goodbye" to Industrial Age thinking.

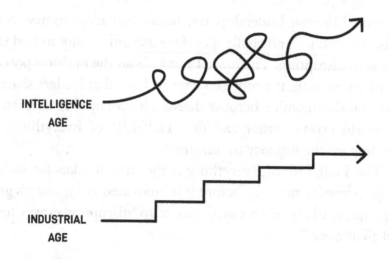

INTELLIGENCE
AGE

INDUSTRIAL
AGE

Industrial Age	Intelligence Age
Managers of tasks	Facilitators of learning
Cultures of conformity	Cultures of curiosity
Supply chains	Supply brains
Profits at any cost	Social and business value
Doing digital	Being digital
Fake empowerment	Trust and autonomy
Economies of scale	Economies of learning
Avoiding failure	Learning from failure
Jobs and careers	Skills and projects
Return on efficiency	Return on intelligence

Source: Hack Future Lab

Stephen Hawking famously observed that "intelligence is the ability to adapt to change." Unlearning is the ultimate form of intelligence for staying ahead of disruption in the Intelligence Age. In the twentieth century, organizations focused on control, efficiency, and economies of scale. Today, in a post-industrial world, the focus is on economies of learning and collective trust. In a rapidly changing environment where company life spans are shortening, leaders must strengthen two types of trust, essential for unlearning: 1. Challenger Trust, showing the courage to call out blind spots, testing old wisdom and certainties, and updating outworn beliefs; and 2. Mission Trust is willing to lead the enterprise as one team and elevate belief and commitment in each other.

Challenger Trust

- Lean into the discomfort of feedback
- Share divergent points of view
- Challenge taken-for-granted norms
- Speak up about issues and call out blind spots
- Shared reality to shape the future

Mission Trust

- Lead the enterprise together
- Align around must-win priorities
- Lead as one unified team
- High execution certainty
- A win together mindset

Mind the Agility Gap

Most organizations list agility as one of their top three strategic priorities, yet according to Hack Future Lab, only 18% describe themselves as having agile-wide behaviors.[5] The agility paradox is one of the reasons why unlearning is the key to pushing the business beyond its usual boundaries, turning risk into reward, and leading change. Without unlearning, leaders are overwhelmed with too many meetings, priorities, and emails that don't harness intelligence or create value. Take so-called "best practices" that no longer function as intended and are now "broken practices," or

KPIs that have reached the end of their usefulness. Yet, we still waste time and energy using them or work cultures that recognize and reward conformity more than courage or curiosity. Enough is enough. We must show willful humility in shedding old beliefs and rejecting zombie leadership, starting with where leaders should invest their time for future readiness. Good leaders learn, but the best leaders unlearn. Here are three practical stories to get the best returns from your unlearning efforts.

1. From bureaucratic bullshit (BS) to extreme ownership

Bureaucratic BS is an age-old challenge that plagues most large organizations. Growth creates bureaucracy, which makes overly centralized, overly bureaucratic, and risk-averse organizations. Too many leaders are drowning in "bureaucratic BS," meaning excess friction: rules, duplicated processes, unnecessary meetings, and silo behaviors that slow down decision-making and ultimately kill innovation. One of our time's most ironic paradoxes is that technology changes fast, but humans don't. Leaders are suffering from a common-sense gap, with bureaucratic BS outstripping our human brains' capacity to make sense of it all, leading to structural stupidity in our organizations and rewards for building fiefdoms of bureaucracy. Take resource allocation: budgets, Opex spending, Capex spending, sales, and marketing dollars. The correlation of the same business allocating roughly the same dollar to the same executives yearly is exceptionally high because bureaucratic BS is sticky like glue, and there's inertia in the system.

Four billion pieces of paper are used daily, and the number of words in the US Tax Code has increased from 400,000 to 4 million in the last 20 years. San Francisco City Hall is pushing a new initiative to speed up its glacial hiring process for city workers, which currently takes an average of 255 days.[6] We move closer to zombie leadership, leading with dead ideas every time we forget to unlearn the old ways, whether attending too many pointless meetings or rules that become the proxy for how we work. Do processes serve us, or do we serve the processes? We stop looking at outcomes and ensure we do the processes right. The role of leaders should not be bureaucracy itself but protecting what creates value and serves the purpose. Every organization would benefit from a bi-yearly Marie Kondo exercise, named after the Netflix star who detoxes and declutters messy homes; all employees need to be responsible for streamlining operations and trimming what authors Gary Hamel and Michele Zanini, of the book *Humanocracy: Creating Organizations as Amazing as the People Inside Them*, call the "Bureaucratic Mass index."[7] Given the high price humans pay in lost time and intelligence doing tasks that don't make a difference, I call it "bureaucratic BS."

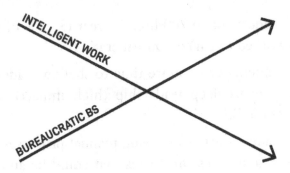

Winning the future is no longer just about scale and efficiency. It's about Return on Intelligence – a cognitively enabled human-led, AI-enabled culture where humans are empowered to solve problems and co-create the future; a collective intelligence enabled by freedom, trust, and responsibility rather than control and bureaucratic BS. Hack Future Lab's research on unlearning confirms that most leaders struggle with record levels of bureaucratic BS, leaving them less willpower to focus on their top priorities. No wonder most leaders can't focus on what matters. Leaders are exhausted. Screen fatigue. Meetings fatigue. Collaboration fatigue. Bureaucratic BS fatigue. With more than $41 trillion of enterprise value at risk from disruption and $17 trillions yearly wasted globally on excess bureaucracy, 93% of leaders believe that excess bureaucracy could be one of the most significant barriers to growth of our times.[8] We have less energy to focus on high-value leadership activities whenever we forget to unlearn the zombie ways, whether too many meetings and emails that make the trivial seem urgent or annual performance reviews that become tick-boxing exercises. Bureaucracy is like costs. They always need to be cut. This is the essence of bureaucratic BS, an insidious corporate disease from which leaders suffer.

Slow, Siloed, and Complicated

- 1/3 of leaders spend 700 hours a year (33.3% of their total hours worked a year) on bureaucratic BS
- 1/3 of leaders devote more time to shallow leadership (low impact) versus deep leadership (high impact) because of bureaucratic BS
- 1/2 of leaders waste time using manual processes, "broken" practices, and excess protocols that could be automated or eliminated
- 1/2 of leaders agree that bureaucratic BS is a "leadership tax" on speed, agility, and talent

Source: Hack Future Lab

The most significant risk to long-term performance, well-being, and resilient growth is not market volatility or the rise of exponential technologies but failure to unlearn excess levels of bureaucratic BS in our organizations that we have normalized. The number one takeaway is that the higher your business's bureaucratic BS level, the *slower* you make decisions, avoid risks, and lead for the future. So, what can you do differently to evolve from a leader of bureaucracy to a leader of contribution?

For each statement, score your bureaucratic BS level on a scale from 1 (low) to 5 (high). A score of 3 or below indicates a priority area for action.

Measure My Bureaucratic BS (Score Yourself on a Scale of 1–5) 5 = "Strongly Agree"

1. Bureaucratic BS slows down decision-making in my organization	1 2 3 4 5
2. I spend too much time attending wasteful meetings	1 2 3 4 5
3. We have too many rules, processes, and protocols	1 2 3 4 5
4. Trust and autonomy are a strength in my organization	1 2 3 4 5
5. We have a culture that rewards bureaucracy over agility	1 2 3 4 5
6. We learn at the speed of the customer	1 2 3 4 5
7. Speed to insights and innovation are optimized	1 2 3 4 5
8. Internal politics is a barrier to making things happen	1 2 3 4 5
9. There are too many manual processes that should be automated	1 2 3 4 5
10. I'm happy with the level of bureaucratic BS in my organization	1 2 3 4 5

The CEO of a large bank (let's call it Alpha) reviewed the results of her firm's annual employee engagement survey and was worried that bureaucratic BS emerged as the number one obstacle to productivity. Among the senior leaders surveyed, 93% agreed with the statement, "We spend too much time on unnecessary bureaucratic activities"; 72% agreed, "We waste too much time on meetings and emails that don't matter," and 29% agreed, "Making high-velocity, high-quality decisions are a strength." The CEO was shocked at the results. Only one-third of the leaders surveyed said that decision-making was a strength. Even worse, most leaders agreed that they devoted most of their energy to activities not focused on sharpening the growth and value agenda, such as project status meetings, email, and bureaucratic BS.

The results of the bureaucratic BS survey are typical in the banking sector and across all industries. Most organizations need to wake up when it comes to learning at the speed of the customer. Hack Future Lab's analysis of hundreds of organizations shows that only 24% of leaders believe they work in agile and future-ready companies, and 79% reveal that bureaucratic BS is the *norm* rather than the exception. This is a terrible indictment of the state of the workplace today, with more than $3 trillion a year wasted in the United States alone on excess bureaucracy. Even the Pentagon has been accused by *The Washington Post* of burying evidence of $125 billion in bureaucratic waste for fear of losing its funding.[9]

When the CEO of Alpha Bank discovered that bureaucratic BS was a clear and present danger to productivity and growth, her first instinct was to schedule more bureaucratic activities such as emails, meetings, and committees to solve the problem. Hack Future Lab's research outlines three counterintuitive strategies to eliminate bureaucratic BS through deliberate and targeted unlearning.

1. Empathy: Acknowledge bureaucratic BS is an issue

Bureaucratic BS happens naturally and increases exponentially because scale and growth create complexity. Too much complexity will undermine any business's capacity to move fast in the long run. Leaders often underestimate the scale of bureaucracy by up to 30%, especially with their direct reports. That significantly affects a team's ability to be entrepreneurial and sustainably deliver breakthrough performance. The worst thing a leader can do is assume we are all on the same page regarding bureaucracy because the likelihood is that bureaucratic BS gets worse the further down the management layers you go. To avoid being misunderstood or seen as not listening, take simple steps with your people to empower everybody to tackle unnecessary bureaucracy and provide the trust and tools to make the unlearning stick. For example, Meta declared the Year of Efficiency, and Google committed to an annual simplification drive to reduce the number of enterprise-wide Objectives and Key Results (OKRs) by a third.[10] Everybody is responsible for eliminating bureaucratic BS in the organization, and recognition is shown when excess bureaucracy is reduced.

2. Activation: Start a quarterly challenge to unlearn responsibly bureaucratic BS

The key to unlearning excess bureaucratic BS is to connect people to unlearning initiatives across the enterprise and mobilize stakeholders to own their part of the unlearning agenda. Leaders can activate the unlearning muscle in everyone by a.) Inviting teams to rank the organization's highest sources of bureaucratic BS, b.) Empower stakeholders to remove zombie practices through ideas such as "Kill a Stupid Rule" and use the unlearning process SEAO: Simplify, Eliminate, Automate, or Outsource, c.) Reinforce and sustain unlearning behaviors by recognizing and celebrating "Unlearning Champions" in the organization and sharing stories of the positive impact that has resulted from their unlearning efforts. Unlearning starts with leadership humility and the psychological capital of knowing our voice matters and that we belong and have a duty of care to replace bureaucratic work with intelligent work.

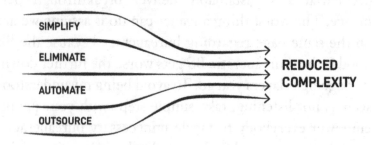

3. Sustain: Reflect and feed-forward to make unlearning stick

Plans inform. Stories inspire and sustain the collective humility to unlearn for the long term. Take bi-yearly bureaucratic BS surveys to ask zombie-busting questions, track quick wins, and ensure that the practice of unlearning becomes part of a broader continuous growth and value agenda and an essential part of what it means to "add" to a high-performing culture.

- What is our median bureaucratic BS score across the business?
- How does our bureaucratic BS score compare to our industry peers?
- What would help us work with focus and clarity?
- Where precisely should we remove bureaucratic BS to get better results?
- What do we unlearn to stay entrepreneurial and focused on agility and growth?

- What are we doing that we should not be doing?
- Are we learning at the speed of the customer? If not, why not?
- Where else should we simplify, eliminate, automate, or outsource our work (SEAO)?

By tackling these questions for unlearning at both the individual and enterprise scale, it becomes clear how interdependent they are and why unlearning bureaucratic BS is more than making work more efficient. The leadership team at Alpha Bank looked at its bureaucratic BS survey results and found conclusively that they needed to be more proactive at pruning costs and reallocating resources to higher yielding and higher growth opportunities. They realized that too much bureaucracy had become invisible to leaders, and it was long overdue to force tough conversations about winning the future together by adopting a shared mindset of reductionism. This disrupting from-the-inside lens looks honestly at the anatomy of how work gets done and uncovers new ways to cut expenses, simplify processes, and innovate faster. It encourages everybody to constantly seek improvement by revisiting fundamental principles about "why we do what we do" and finding innovative ways to optimize productivity and well-being. The lesson for Alpha Bank is that everybody is responsible for reducing bureaucratic BS, and this should be transparent and measured alongside growth and profitability.

Failure to Reimagine Failure

"If you want to be successful, I would encourage you to grow a tolerance for failure," says NVIDIA's CEO Jensen Huang.[11] How would you rate your tolerance for failure? It's a question I was asked during a leadership conference I was speaking at, which forced me to reflect on how we often miss the upside of failure because there is no learning without failing, and there is no progress without setbacks. Failing well means failure is productive and helps us improve because there are always lessons in our losses. You don't assign self-worth to something that didn't work out, and you can confidently move forward. Looking back, I've been terrible at learning to fail well. Ego, embarrassment, or a lack of curiosity often got in the way. Maybe I'm a failure pioneer, but you must decide what constitutes failure. One extensive data study of more than 30 years of VC investment found a prior failure to be "the essential prerequisite for success." The key is learning from each mistake. The top scorers in the Premier League miss half their shots, and basketball players know that the best way to become a great player is to learn from the misses. Like leaders and teams, great players sometimes miss the ball, shake their heads, and move on.[12]

I've had my fair share of failures. I've had failed relationships, interviews, projects, and dreams, although I did pass my driving test the first time. I don't think it's possible to have any life or be a leader if you're not prepared to take a courageous leap into the unknown and lean into the discomfort of failure. A helpful question is, "How do we learn and grow from failure and use it to shape who we become?" Sara Blakely, the founder of the lifestyle brand Spanx, says, "When my brother and I were growing up, my father would encourage us to fail. We'd sit around the dinner table, and he'd ask, 'What did you guys fail at this week?' If we had nothing to tell him, he'd be disappointed. The logic seems counterintuitive, but it worked beautifully. He knew that many people become paralyzed by the fear of failure. They're constantly afraid of what others will think if they don't do a great job and, as a result, take no risks. My father wanted us to try everything and feel free to push the envelope. His attitude taught me to define failure as not trying something I want to do instead of not achieving the right outcome."

On the other side of failure is its closest cousin, learning, followed by resilience, the capacity to bounce back from challenges. Hack Future Lab's research shows that the best organizations don't just react to crises. They use them as a platform to get wiser and more agile and turn barriers into upside. For example, failure can help us manage overconfidence in an idea or decision. Post-mortems can help leaders get more thoughtful about the scaffolding behind their thinking rather than settle scores about failure. We often find ourselves reluctant to confront failure, as it is a human instinct. The purpose of a post-mortem should primarily be focused on gathering information and using it for proactive resilience-building and humility to rethink and unlearn, treat it as valuable insights, and examine it without blaming others.[13]

The ancient Stoics were right. Never waste a good mistake and start before you're ready or risk not starting. I've concluded that the biggest failure is not learning from failure. I have found this to be the case when I work with teams in organizations worldwide and ask them, "What risks are we okay with?" Many have not discussed a "productive risk or failure" and how that may fuel greater results; they are 100% risk-averse, full stop. Why do leaders and their teams fear risks and failures, and what practical steps can we take to unlearn to avoid failure and learn to fail well?

A Brief History of Failure

Let's do a simple test. If I say "failure," what words come into your mind? Loser. Nobody. Lazy. Write off. If failure were a brand, it would probably fail, yet to be human is to fail, and to fail is to be human. Unlearning our fear of failure is one of the best ways to sustain long-term vitality and remain future-ready in the face of value chain disintermediation, new disruptive technologies, and changing customer preferences. Culture and context matter, but learning to fail well is a multiplier for resiliency, new ideas, and fostering a curiosity-led culture; indeed, as Amazon founder Jeff Bezos says: "Failure and invention are inseparable twins. At Amazon, we must grow the size of our failures as our company grows. We have to make bigger and bigger failures – otherwise, none of our failures will be needle movers. Over the long run, it would be a bad sign if Amazon didn't make larger failures. Doing that all along the way will protect you from ever having to make that big Hail Mary bet that you sometimes see companies make right before they fail or go out of existence."[14] Learning to fail well is no longer a nice to have. When the ratio of knowing to uncertainty is high, learning from failures can help leaders reduce uncertainty about the future and be ready to grab new opportunities before they become mainstream.

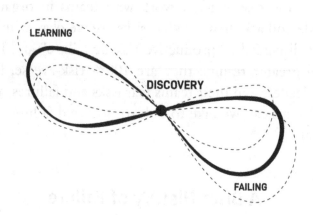

Most of us don't view challenges as opportunities for growth, failures as lessons, or feedback as a pathway to improvement. We struggle to overcome the failure paradox, which means that organizations can't innovate without failing but can't fail without innovating. Hack Future Lab's research on learning to fail well shows that:

- 67% of teams agree fear of failure is the norm in their organizations
- 53% of leaders tolerate small-scale failure
- 46% of leaders encourage dissent and debate
- 27% of leaders recognize and reward learning from productive failures

Source: Hack Future Lab

One of the most significant challenges for unlearning the fear of failure is that we are hard-wired from an early age to avoid risk and change. The curiosity to learn and the courage to fail well by deliberately learning from failure are squeezed out of us like lemons as we leave college and move into the workforce. No wonder leaders become failure avoiders, afraid of failure, and misunderstanding that there are different kinds of failure, including ones with an upside. There is a societal aversion to failing and a perception that failure is a badge of shame when it should be a badge of courage.

Re-perception – the ability to see, hear, or become aware of something new in existing information and notice our organizational, leadership, or cultural blind spots – is at the heart of failing well. It's encouraging, therefore, to see that even central banks worldwide, including the Fed, ECB, and BOE, are rethinking their forecasting approach and deliberately learning from their mistakes in underestimating inflation badly in the last few years. The ECB's president, Christine Lagarde, says: "We should have learned that we cannot rely only on textbook cases and pure models. We have to think with a broader horizon."[15] After several high-profile failures to spot recent inflationary spikes, it's a moment of collective humility by central banks to reimagine their economic forecasting models and prioritize a culture of learning over "knowing." Leaders must constantly challenge taken-for-granted norms in a rapidly changing environment where the "half-life" of everything is a given.

As central banks have realized, the avoid-failure mindset hampers our capacity to learn from failure and is ultimately a future readiness bottleneck. I believe today's operating environment of new competitors, new technologies, and new customers demands that we reframe failure and recognize that risk and reward are inseparable; we can't have one without the other, which is how the universe is wired. If leaders want to find the upside in disruption, failure is part of the journey, so how do we break free from the avoid-failure mindset, and what's the difference between a productive failure and an unproductive one?

From Action, I Learn (FAIL)

Not all risks or failures are created equal. A productive failure is typically hypothesis-driven and can help reduce uncertainty by providing new insight, lessons, or game-changing discoveries to help leaders turn obstacles into opportunities. Take the discovery of graphene, the world's thinnest material. It is a wonder material that is only one atom thick, 1 million times thinner than human hair, but more robust than steel or diamonds. Two researchers at The University of Manchester, Professor Andre Geim and Professor Kostya Novoselov, frequently held "Friday night experiments" – playful meetings where they would test and experiment with ideas and put productive failures to work in a meaningful way. One Friday, the two scientists observed after a failed experiment that some flakes from a bulk of graphite were left on sticky tape. By repeatedly separating the graphite fragments, they could create flakes just one atom thick, inadvertently leading to the discovery of isolated graphene for the first time. What started as an accidental failure has led to a new way of thinking about materials and limitless potential for the future. Even failures can be instructive sometimes.[16]

Chefs, artists, scientists, and inventors understand the power of learning to fail well. They know that FAIL stands for "From Action I Learn." They are curiosity-driven problem solvers exploring the edges of their comfort zones and asking mindset-shifting questions that don't just make them feel good but make them think hard. Ask yourself, "What you intended to happen, what happened, and what lessons can be learned from your failure?" The best way to fail well is to invest time and intelligence in continuous learning, learning the good, the bad, and the ugly lessons, and rejecting the zombie idea that we can innovate without failing.

An unproductive failure is the opposite, and circumstances matter. It is caused by inattention, carelessness, or avoidable errors that waste energy and time. Sometimes, an unproductive failure is more significant than the sum of its parts and is attributable to a broader cultural failure; sometimes, it can prove fatal. The Boeing MAX 737 crisis is a tragic story and a crucial lesson for leaders about disregarding the opportunity to learn from failure after two planes crashed, claiming more than 340 lives. The pressure to rush a product to market and chase financial performance before engineering excellence meant shortcuts were taken and avoidable risks were missed. Among the internal documents was a comment from an employee who said the 737 MAX was "designed by clowns, who in turn are supervised by monkeys," while another claimed they wouldn't put their family on one of the planes.[17] Like any employee from any organization, Boeing's employees needed to be recognized and rewarded for identifying concerns or inevitable failures about the airplane's design and safety issues before they occurred.

To prepare better for unproductive failures and protect continuous listening and feedback loops that act as early internal warning systems, teams need the trust and autonomy to take pre-mortems, reflect on what is missing, and rank the issues in order of risk. After, identify the best ways of eliminating the risks and increasing the chances of a successful and productive outcome. Ask, "Imagine that we have failed. What would be the reasons for that failure, and what can we do today to avoid this from happening?" Recognize and celebrate failure role models who speak up about their setbacks and have shared the lessons with others and avoid knee-jerk reactions of disappointment or "shame and blame" when things go wrong. There are many upsides to learning to fail well. We must decide what constitutes a productive failure, which is better done as a group. The world is eager to give us a set of criteria for success and failure if we let it. Failure means stripping away the inessential. Without learning to fail well, there's no humility and no evolution. Hack Future Lab's research shows that another helpful starting point for learning to fail well is to ask questions that cultivate trust and belief in each other.

1. Thinking about our role as leaders, what's eroding?

2. Do we model "learning to fail well" mindsets and behaviors?

3. Do we minimize or maximize risk and reward?

4. Do we frame work as learning goals?

5. Do we recognize and celebrate productive failures?

6. Do we obsess over trust and values, not just metrics?

7. Is speaking up a strength?

8. Do we have a culture of curiosity (embracing risk and ideas that challenge the status quo) or a culture of conformity (rejecting ideas that challenge the status quo)?

9. Do we have leaders of learning or leaders of defending the status quo?

10. Do we use the right metrics and OKRs to track productive failures?

Sherlock Holmes famously said once to his friend Watson: "You see, but you do not observe. The distinction is clear." Leaders who are facilitators of learning to fail well help others go beyond seeing to *observing* their blind spots to failure; they help others step out of their comfort zones and avoid zombie zones where dead ideas and assumptions live on. People feel more alive and empowered to serve the purpose, trust each other, and solve problems. Organizations are better prepared for the future and critically show more collective humility, a powerful safeguard against complacency or hubris.

A Story of Unlearning a Toxic Culture

Culture has a collective action problem: Culture is everyone's and no one's problem. What don't we know about our organizational cultures, and why don't we know it? Agnotology studies cultural or ethical blind spots, deceit, ignorance, and why knowing sometimes does not come to be or becomes invisible, which is central to our final story of unlearning.[18] Uber is a ride-hailing firm with a market cap of more than $120 billion and around

23,000 employees worldwide. I remember the first time I requested an Uber ride on my app in 2011. I was in New York on my way to a meeting in Chelsea on 75 Ninth Avenue and stood on a street corner holding out my hand, hoping the iconic yellow cab would see me and stop. I suddenly realized that I had no dollar notes on me and that I would have to go to an ATM to get money to pay for the cab fare. And then it started raining. Uber changed everything with an ambitious mission to reimagine the future of mobility, logistics, and delivery services. First, it increased demand for the sharing economy, such as companies like Airbnb or DoorDash, Inc., as an alternative to traditional channels. It showed how competitive lines and customer behaviors are redefined and how quickly asset-light, tech-enabled strategies disrupt industries. Uber would become known as the number one disruptor of its time, but at what price?

The difficulty in finding a cab on a snowy night in Paris inspired the original idea for Uber, and following a beta launch in May 2010, the Uber mobile app launched publicly in San Francisco in 2011 to much fanfare. As Uber scaled at breakneck speed, a manager sent colleagues a message highlighting Silicon Valley's rogue spirit of "move fast and break things": "Embrace the chaos. It means you're doing something meaningful."[19] Uber quickly became the poster child for unprofitable tech companies during record low-interest rates and more than $20 billion of funding from investors, including Softbank Group Corp., Benchmark Capital, and Microsoft co-founder Bill Gates. Uber's culture, during its years of explosive growth, would constantly come under the spotlight with allegations of wasteful spending, bullying, and a toxic "bro culture." By 2019, "the embrace the chaos" mantra of playing loose with the rules had resulted in an operating loss of $8.5 billion (£6.8 billion) on revenue of just $14.1 billion and a series of whistleblower scandals and regulatory investigations that led to a change at the top.[20]

Under the leadership of CEO Dara Khosrowshahi, Uber has evolved from a culture of "move fast and break things" to "move fast and do the right thing" and is prioritizing the needs of its customers and employees alongside growth, scale, and profit. Through deliberate unlearning of a toxic culture over time, and despite operating at a loss for nearly 14 years, Uber 2.0 has led a significant overhaul of its culture and helped it reach its first operating profit. Uber's story underlines the need for steep learning curves, difficult choices, and ethical leadership at every turn. Here are three leadership lessons to unlearn a toxic culture and shape a better one where trust, equity, and integrity are our North Star.

- **Silence breakers:** When's the last time you wanted to speak up about an idea, concern, or question but stayed quiet because of fear? Or worked in a corrosive culture where challenging the status quo was too risky? Hack Future Lab's research shows that one-third of the global workforce chooses silence over speaking up in a meeting or one-to-one every month. Cultures differ when confronting issues, but the takeaway is that silence is always less risky than speaking up, and cultures of "SEP" (somebody else's problem) are the norm rather than the exception. A culture of conformity deters people from speaking up and is a "courage to unlearn" wrecker. It demands compliance and deference and is better suited to command and coerce leadership styles during General Napoleon's reign.

  Leaders' alarm bells should be ringing if they have a culture of avoidance. Your organization's return on intelligence, psychological safety capital, and trust are low, and opportunities and talent are wasted. Every organization needs courageous "silence breakers" at every level, including the boardroom, to answer the question, "What needs to be said that is not being said?" At Uber, asking this question has led to the unlearning of its brash cultural values, ditching ones like "toe-stepping" and "Always be hustling" to "Do the right thing" and "We celebrate difference." The new set of human-led values is for a responsible firm that doesn't just focus ruthlessly on "growth at any costs" but is more reflective of a future-fit, purpose-driven, and values-led leadership. Nothing is easy when unlearning a toxic culture. However, paying attention to the correct values and tone at the top is an excellent way to get started, and silence breakers across the organization are essential.

- **It takes a village:** Missteps and a series of cultural short-comings set the tone for Uber at the beginning of its heady growth, and, more recently, regulators are investigating the Big Four consulting and accounting firms to rethink governance, strengthening oversight, and holding management to account.[21] Too much leadership today is the same old things in the same way, and too many people are disengaged at work. Unlearning a toxic culture allows everyone to break out of their echo chambers and challenge established beliefs and assumptions about why and how leaders operate. It's the difference between creating an environment where truth, trust, and transparency exist, not a toxic and complacent one.

  First, when everyone is working on behalf of the culture and strategy daily, leadership should work more closely as one unified team with a laser-like focus on strengthening who we are, how we work, and how we grow. Too many one-to-one relationships can erode collective trust and under-mine commitment and alignment around the must-win priorities. Machiavellian principles where "the end justifies the means" become the leadership code for making deci-sions. Formal training, especially for first-time managers, can help build an honest, not feared culture. For example, both Uber and Disney have introduced Corporate Universities to get all the employees on the same wavelength when it comes to mission, culture, and values but also make the programs sustainable by avoiding knee-jerk reactions to doing an "event" rather than creating a journey that encourages reflection, action, and personal empowerment for the long term.[22]

- **Make time to unlearn a culture:** If culture is important, why don't leaders make enough time for it? It takes discipline to build a healthy, trust-based culture rather than a fear-based one, and it should prompt leaders to rethink how best to hold themselves accountable in the boardroom. The challenge is that when firms scale up fast, the leadership team becomes increasingly detached from the rest of the organization. This misalignment can cause the leaders to overestimate what's going well and underestimate what isn't. Hubris becomes an existential risk, and values can lose their meaning. Independent non-executive directors and externally appointed chairs are essential for scrutinizing decisions, but that's not enough, and many firms have yet to accept how much involvement the non-execs need to have to make a visible difference. It is far better to acknowledge a gap and listen and inspire others to own their part of the unlearning agenda and feel set up for success without the exercise becoming a tick-boxing one. To make a turnaround at Uber, internal cheerleaders such as Harvard Professor Frances Frei showed a willingness to call out problems, engage in constructive debate, and connect people to deeply personalized unlearning initiatives that made it crystal clear that every individual has a right to own their part of the culture because in the end "who we are is what we say and do."[23]

Unlearning Is the Answer

Companies have reached an inflection point in their growth narratives. As leaders pivot to an AI-enabled future, there is fear and excitement, but is enough being done to unlearn "the always-done ways" and avoid zombie leadership? The short answer is no. We know the world and its leadership are not in good shape, and the numbers tell the story:

- 81% of workers believe stress, overwork, and burnout have worsened in the last year
- 77% of workers are worried about the rise of AI and its impact on jobs
- 66% of workers believe companies aren't doing enough to make their business models and supply chains sustainable
- 57% of workers say "they're over-managed and under-led"
- 48% of workers believe they get to put their best skills to work every day
- 34% of workers go to work scared or anxious

Source: Hack Future Lab

Unlearning is not a quick fix for the dire state of leadership, and there is no one-size-fits-all strategy to prepare for the future of work; however, leaders should consider several unlearning themes to strengthen their future readiness muscle. The old leadership paradigms are eroding, and it's up to leaders to adapt, too.

- **Future-readiness:** All leaders must prioritize unlearning, including concrete unlearning OKRs, because it's the cornerstone of future readiness and long-term resilient growth. It is a proven way to replace over-confidence with rethinking and humility cycles. IKEA started questioning revenue forecasting, something they have no control over, instead of forecasting spending and investment where there is control. It ditched its traditional annual budget forecasts, replacing them with scenario plans that allow managers to adapt as circumstances dictate. Instead of setting specific goals for the year, it has a set of "scenarios" to give the business wiggle room as the outlook changes.[24] It's teaching humility and agility and reclaiming lost time to re-focus on the growth pillars of innovation, talent, and customers. IKEA started its unlearning journey by asking, "What unlearning would help us lead better to serve our teams and customers?" "Where should we remove obstacles to get better results faster, and what do we unlearn to reduce bureaucratic BS and stay nimble and focused as we grow?"

- **Lousy meetings:** "This meeting could have been an email" is a thought that every leader thinks about most days, and that's why the way we run meetings must be unlearned. Unproductive meetings cost organizations billions in lost productivity and employee time. In the United States alone, wasteful meetings cost firms more than $100 billion annually in lost productivity, according to Hack Future Lab.[25] The biggest reasons cited for futile meetings are no agenda, late arrivals, and the wrong attendees at the meeting. Shopify, a Canadian e-commerce firm, set out to unlearn lousy meetings by asking employees which activities they invest time and energy in that should be eliminated. The answer was unequivocal: "Too many meetings."

Agility is a mental tool that can be improved, but leaders are overloaded with last-minute meetings that waste time and money. Strategic focus suffers, and attention spans become fragmented, impacting pace and execution certainty.

No wonder two-thirds of leaders believe that they don't have enough time in the day to execute their top strategic priorities because of lousy meetings. While not without controversy, the unlearning goal of eliminating the number of pointless meetings by introducing a meeting cost calculator across the business has been a success at Shopify. The average cost of a 30-minute meeting with three employees can be $1,600, but an executive in the meeting can go up to $2,000. The new tool, which shows on employees' calendars, estimates how much a meeting will cost the business based on the number of attendees and average compensation data across roles and departments. Shopify's experiment has been an enormous success; the average time spent in meetings is down more than 20% for each employee, and more than 20,000 meetings were removed in the first few months of its rollout.[26]

Over-managed and under-led: While employees worldwide are rethinking their purpose at work, leaders must also be prepared to unlearn ways of leading to ensure the highest levels of clarity, growth, and belonging in their teams. I had a boss named The Shadow during my early career working in consulting. When my boss entered the room, the temperature would drop, and I would feel a cold shiver run down my spine. A few moments later, my boss would be next to me, whispering, "What are you doing, Terence?" At that moment, my boss thought he was coaching me. He was "checking." It was terrifying. Hack Future Lab's research shows that after health and family, the number one driver of life satisfaction is the quality of our relationship with our direct boss. The bad news is that 66% of employees agree that their boss is the number one source of anxiety and that the way many of us lead is ripe for change.[27]

Several leadership styles are evolving to reflect what's new and what's next in leadership and performance management, which is a hedge against the risk of becoming a zombie leader.

- From infrequent evaluator to continuous coaching
- From talent hoarding to talent sharing
- From fake empowerment to freedom and responsibility
- From transactional to transformational interactions
- From command and control to care and co-creation
- From hierarchies of authority to networks of agility

How do we make our leadership sustainable, inclusive, and resilient? Most organizations fall short when asking what's evolving and eroding in their leadership style. I was invited to join a Nordic Business Forum webinar about the future of leadership and how many leaders are grappling with wildly different leadership styles.[28] Leading at the edge of uncertainty, unlearning becomes vital. Leaders must strengthen their context-setting, trust-building, and pacesetting capabilities to create an irresistible and shared reality of the future and say goodbye to "checking over coaching" and embarrassing "feedback sandwiches."

Unlearning Equals Agility and Humility

Without a commitment to unlearning, expertise and assumptions quickly become obsolete, and we become prisoners of the mental models and habits of our past success. It erodes future readiness and can weigh us down. The Japanese word Henka (変化) means embracing evolution and rethinking in cycles; it's inspired by nature and is the antidote to becoming slow, siloed, and bureaucratic.

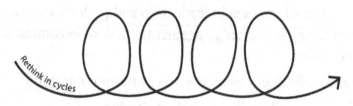

EMBRACE EVOLUTION

Rethink in cycles

Henka is like turning lead into gold or oil into water. In true Henka spirit, unlearning is the ultimate agility advantage and a must-have skill to be cultivated and practiced in a focused way. It matters because the future isn't just about strategy and execution. Unlearning strengthens our future readiness muscle, a vastly underutilized skill set in organizations today, and helps us prepare for finding the upside in disruption.

Takeaways

- **Champion unlearning:** A lot of the drive to unlearn at an enterprise level requires people to give up old ways and try new ones. At NASA, every day, leaders ask, "Are we learning at the speed of science? If not, why not?" Unlearning is essential to innovation – it brings new and unexpected ideas necessary during accelerating change. As the rate of disruption accelerates, so must the rate of learning and relearning, pushing the organization outside its comfort zone. At NASA, leaders expect others to unlearn taken-for-granted norms by sharing the stories of the positive impact that has resulted from its unlearning actions. For example, a 30-Day Unlearn Challenge helps to simplify, eliminate, automate, or outsource broken activities that no longer serve the mission. NASA leaders ask, "Which activities do we invest time and intelligence in that should be eliminated?" and "What do we unlearn in our team and organization to fully operate at our highest potential?" Bold questions help NASA teams see the future through multiple lenses; they know the best way to stay relevant is to normalize unlearning as one half of success where everybody is trusted to question zombie practices and challenge outdated assumptions that: 1. No longer are true, and 2. Don't add value.[29]

- **FAIL (From Action I Learn):** To avoid the "shame & blame trap," jazz players have a sublime turn of phrase for learning from failure – "say yes to the mess." It's a mindset of radical receptivity and a spirit of humility to lean into the discomfort of risk and failure. In 2012, Canva founder Melanie Perkins had to lead herself through failure. She was rejected by investors more than 100 times. "Each of those rejections hurt," she said. She waited three more years for the first investment. Canva is now worth $25 billion. Success and failure go hand in hand and are the spark for developing courageous thinkers and doers.[30] In a rapidly changing world, we must avoid "performative leadership" and fear of failure to sustain long-term vitality and be ready to adapt to anything. Leaders can help others unlearn their fear of failure by exploring the team's collective beliefs and experiences about the idea of failure, ranging from "failure must be avoided at all costs" to "fail fast to learn fast." To reframe failure as a badge of respect, not shame, we should acknowledge that most failures offer learning opportunities and that the worst type of failure is not learning from failing.

Questions to ask include:

- What are examples of productive versus unproductive failures in our organization?

- How do we reskill from avoiding failure to being hypothesis-driven and taking smart risks?

- What concrete steps can we take today to reward and recognize productive failures in our team?

    The key is prioritizing action over overthinking and, like the jazz players, saying "yes to the mess" and learning from the mess.

- **Fight bureaucratic BS:** The biggest risk to the long-term survival of most companies is not external threats such as competitors or market disruption. It's internal risks from bureaucratic BS and the normalization of bureaucratic over intelligent work. Bureaucratic BS is a significant internal barrier to growth, and employees agree, ranking bureaucratic BS as the number one barrier to productivity. As organizations become more bureaucratic, there's a leadership bias to manage more proxies and "battles among the silos." Bureaucratic work becomes essential in business at the expense of ideas, innovation, and leading change. This leads to an "organizational tragedy of the commons," where individuals inadvertently produce collective harm. The higher the bureaucratic BS, the slower the organization becomes. Inertia. Excuses and procrastination are the norm, and as such, sap initiative and drive. Leaders stop looking at results or outcomes and fixate on teams doing the process right.

    The process becomes "the thing," and bureaucracy becomes the strategy. The organizational chart of the 1850s, which had a hierarchy at its core, is no longer relevant. We need to build for communities, not for hierarchies. At Bayer, the pioneering biopharma firm uses a Dynamic Shared Ownership model (DSO) to maximize a bootstrap ethic and nimble management: flat, fast, and iterative despite legacy and complexity. If it were a formula, it would read "Leadership = trust + freedom × ownership." Employees are expected to put common sense *over* bureaucracy and democratize ideas and decisions by asking, "Do our rules, meetings, and processes serve or sabotage us? Do we reward and incentivize bureaucratic work and behaviors (doing things right) more than curiosity over conformity (doing the smart thing)?" If the answer is "yes," it's time to simplify, eliminate, automate, or outsource (SEAO). Too many firms suffer "addition sickness" with people adding more friction and slowing thinking and decision-making. "If you want to be a large company and not a dinosaur, you have to find a way to evolve quickly, to adapt, to change, to reinvent yourself," says Bill Anderson, the CEO of Bayer.[31] The lesson is that we are all responsible for reducing friction and rigid hierarchies to embrace the future and stay ahead of change.

Risk: The Courage Advantage

"The real risk is doing nothing."

                                        – **Denis Waitley**

The Consumer Electronics Show (CES) celebrates all that tech offers and sets the technology narrative for the year ahead. Every year, more than one hundred thousand people arrive at the Las Vegas Convention Center to discover the latest innovation trends across the future of consumer tech: AI, robotics, mobile, gaming, and many other tech themes that will reshape how we live, work, and play. I saw an all-electric flying car prototype and a new personal assistant to perform your tasks during my visit. The Rabbit R1 A1 device swaps out apps for an operating system that can learn how to use apps on your behalf and shows how an AI co-pilot could work if you've dreamed of a personal assistant. As I experimented with the device, a man beside me smiled and said, "Cool product. I'm interested in this kind of innovation for my industry." Curious to understand more, I replied, "It's a useful device. Which industry are you working in?" He smiled, "I work in the funeral industry. I'm a funeral director. Our clients want us to be more innovative. If we don't embrace the future, we become history." After my surprise, we spoke for 30 minutes about how the $20 billion a year US funeral industry is evolving from live streaming and space burials to eco-friendly and digital memorials. As we said our goodbyes, I felt nothing but respect for the funeral director. No industry is immune from the forces of disruption – not even death.

One of the most significant risks to the long-term vitality of most companies isn't tech disruption. It's a lack of courage to evolve. For instance, the huge consumer inertia to leave the iPhone and the wider Apple ecosystem works in Apple's favor, and its continuous renewal strategy has served it well, too. Apple watches outsell the Swiss watch industry, yet we're entering a new era of perpetual upheaval where competitive lines are redrawn at the speed of AI.

For Apple and any other incumbent, there are clear warning signs. One is OpenAI's plan for a "GPT store" – a place for developers to sell AI-powered services built on top of OpenAI's models. This platform for supercharged apps looks like a direct challenge to Apple's App Store. Or how about a head-to-head battle between ChatGPT Search and Google? Hack Future Lab's research shows that a "lack of boldness" is the number one barrier to long-term growth, and employees agree, ranking lack of courage as a top three internal challenge alongside bureaucracy and talent scarcity. Future-fit leaders must embrace "The Courage Advantage" to thrive in a new era of perpetual organizational upheaval.

In the opening lines of *A Tale of Two Cities* by Charles Dickens, he writes, "It was the best of times. It was the worst of times. It was the age of wisdom. It was the age of foolishness." Dickens's words seem remarkably prescient for today's business environment of enormous risk, but they also reward those who know how to find the upside in disruption. Change can be challenging, but times of volatility also give us a unique opportunity to rethink and emerge stronger together.

Courage is crucial to speed and agility, too. A client in the insurance sector highlighted that two-thirds of their leaders believed some of its functions had become "blockers to our strategic transformation," and less than "half of the workforce believed intelligent risk-taking was a strength." Compared with peers in slow-moving companies, Hack Future Lab's research shows that courageous leaders in fast-moving organizations report 2.4 times higher operational resilience, 2.2 times higher growth, and 3.7 times higher innovation.[1]

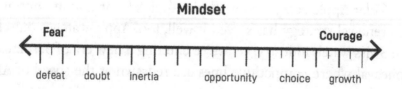

Mindset

Fear → Courage

defeat   doubt   inertia   opportunity   choice   growth

The best protection against downside surprises is to make bold moves. Being bold is not about being reckless or rash but about taking intelligent risks and making tough decisions amidst volatility. It's proactive resilience: faster decisions are often better ones, too. Bold doesn't always mean big, either. Bold can start small. Maya Angelou said, "I realized one isn't born with courage. One develops it by doing small courageous things." Bold leadership begins from within and derives from the Latin word core, which is the heart to speak one's mind by telling one's heart. So, courage is your heart. It takes courage to build a new business or abandon an old one. It takes courage to say goodbye to the status quo. Today, courage is more likely to be effective if it is flexible, nuanced, and contextual. Psychological capital matters, too. With economic headwinds and AI disruption an everyday reality, the answer to disruption is to sharpen the courage advantage, moving from "fear and doubt" to "dare and evolve." Bold leaders don't just scale back during tough times. Instead, they prioritize; they choose. They act. The courage advantage means executing for today and adapting for tomorrow and is one of the most underutilized mindsets and skill sets today.

How does Microsoft dramatically outperform its peers? Once seen as trailing behind in the AI and cloud computing race, the firm has undergone a remarkable transformation marked by a strategic shift to a "Mobile First, Cloud First" firm and a cultural shift emphasizing a growth mindset where different ideas can thrive, and failure is a lever for rapid learning. Transforming pre-emptively before a performance gap occurs has allowed it to explore bold moves for future readiness and from a position of relative strength. Their leaders intentionally and consistently anticipate trends and have learned new mental models to seize the future boldly. Microsoft's revenue per employee is 1.8 times that of Salesforce and far above that of its competitors, and its growth and profitability have made it a $3 trillion-plus market-cap firm.[2]

Bold moves, decisive commitment, and lightspeed execution matter and can help leaders take advantage of volatility and use it as an impetus for finding new paths to growth. Despite a success story like Microsoft, fewer than 20% of companies operate this way, according to McKinsey's estimates. Profitable growth doesn't happen overnight, either. It takes time to achieve and sustain, even in the best times. In the last decade, one in eight companies in the S&P 500 gained 10% annual growth, and 1 in 10 maintained growth rates above GDP growth for more than 30 years.[3] The barriers to sustainable growth include outdated industrial leadership mindsets, old performance and talent management models, and a need for bold leadership.

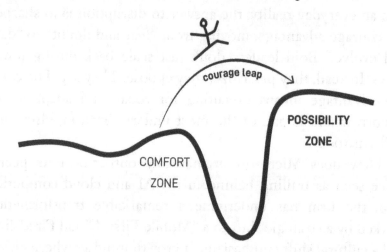

How do you seize the future boldly? It starts with courage leaps, replacing fear with action and doubt with conviction. If you think courage is risky, try a weak strategy or no leadership. Like an action movie, the future demands boldness in who we are, how we lead, and how we grow, especially under pressure. It took 13 days for the British government to learn of the assassination of a US president, as it did of Lincoln's death in 1865.

Today, our decision loops are faster and shorter, requiring answers to difficult but important questions.

- How do we turn disruption into a tailwind for strategic courage?
- How do we solve the Productivity Paradox?
- What's our strategy to harness the powers of AI while managing the risks?
- How do we sharpen our execution muscle?
- How do we lead the future together as one team?
- What new mindsets, cultures, and capabilities will give us a sustainable edge?
- What do we rethink or unlearn to go 10 times wiser or bolder?
- How do we lead the future with bold intentionality?

When your competitors have a courage advantage, they make decisions faster because courage is 80% culture and 20% process. Finding agility means showing the courage to give power back to employees, empowering them to make decisions and co-create the future. Companies leading the way, such as Haier, Nucor, and Spotify, are developing adaptive operating models defined by networks of self-managing teams, rapid decision-making cycles, and a relentless focus on removing barriers to speed and execution.[4] The most courageous firms have created a new leadership edge.

They can act more quickly, mobilize talent and resources, win new customers, and are more resilient in the face of shocks and setbacks. Will average firms ever be able to catch up? Hack Future Lab's research shows that when employees strongly agree that "my organization prioritizes courage over conformity," there is a courage "dividend" too.

The Courage Dividend

- **Leadership evolution:** Evolve from Industrial Age to Intelligence Age thinking

- **Bridging divides:** Foster trust and unity through bold, intentional conversations

- **Macro over micro:** Shift mindsets from "yes, but" to "yes, and"

Source: Hack Future Lab

Courage Calling

When you think about it, change is a leader's calling to find the upside in disruption and turn barriers into breakthroughs. There is a natural Darwinian logic to what the Austrian economist Joseph Schumpeter called the "gales of creative destruction."[5] Disruption always presents a choice: 1. Opportunity if disruption is managed as a *tailwind* or 2. Obsolescence if disruption is dismissed as a headwind. Leaders are surrounded by risks that will shape the future: geopolitical risk, a technology super cycle, cybercrime, supply chain disruption, social instability, deglobalization, and talent scarcity. Disruptions are often interconnected, but there is an upside, too. Disruption can create new but difficult-to-predict opportunities for innovation and transformation. Leaders, therefore, must navigate these disruptions with strategic foresight and courage and demonstrate ambidexterity: careful at managing the downside while boldly prioritizing the upside.

John Deere is a story of steep learning curves, difficult choices, and the courage to lean into the future. Deere started nearly two centuries ago between the Napoleonic Wars and the American Civil War. The US-based manufacturing giant is best known for inventing the steel plow in 1837, and today, it is a world leader in agriculture, forestry, and roadbuilding equipment.[6] With a market cap of more than $100 billion, it's the world's 127th most valuable firm, with a long legacy of partnerships, investments, and acquisitions.[7] One of the most significant risks to a firm's future success is its existing success. The success paradox describes how forces that propel organizations to unusual success are the same forces that drag them down into the abyss. While it's true that historically, firms could exploit existing strengths and defend market positions for many decades, renewing a firm's lease on the future now happens in shorter cycles, and competitive advantage is only temporary. General Electric reached its highest market capitalization during the dot.com bubble, at more than $500 billion. Yet, today, it is valued at $140 billion.[8] In comparison, the 166-year-old Swiss bank Credit Suisse was once valued at more than $100 billion before a series of scandals and missteps saw its collapse and subsequent sale to rival UBS for just $3.3 billion.[9]

Three-quarters of the world's $100 trillion in gross domestic product comprises traditional legacy industries such as manufacturing, transportation, and logistics that have yet to be profoundly transformed by technology.[10] To avoid falling prey to the success trap, the leadership team at John Deere looked at some emerging issues that might shape its future, such as rising labor costs, persistent supply chain issues, and ambitious sustainability goals for the industrial sector. Several business ideas emerged, with Deere making bold moves into autonomous tractors, carbon capture, robots, and drones; and they are exploring patents for a "robot-bee" that can potentially pollinate fields one day. Deere is committed to sharpening its courage advantage by spearheading advances in tech and talent. As a former supply chain policy advisor, Elizabeth Reynolds, says: "Technology innovation around re-industrialization is very different, and we are on the cusp of a real revolution in that area." Indeed, I think we may be at a pivot point, like in 2007. Back then, the introduction of the iPhone led to massive growth in consumer technology. The "app economy" evolved and changed how we communicate, work, play, and shop. Business is about to go through something similar: a long-anticipated shift sped up by decoupling, the pandemic, and the war in Ukraine. It's a transformation that will change the nature of our economy.[11]

In addition to foresight and profitability, Deere has shown anticipation and courage, all underpinned by bold leadership. It demonstrated a rare skill where most leaders' attention is drowning in technology and geopolitical risks: not just protecting a legacy but using it as a platform to reposition itself as a business of the future.

So, what are Deere's courage advantage lessons, and how can any leader harness them as tailwinds for building a resilient and sustainable future? Three bold imperatives are crucial to unlocking the courage advantage in any organization.

1. **Execution certainty:** An everyday leadership blind spot in any organization is "If only we knew what we know." Insights and game-changing ideas often lie hidden in quiet cul-de-sacs around the organization, yet they can create an edge. Belief perseverance is another risky leadership blind spot. In this case, leaders cling to a belief about the future despite new facts that firmly contradict it. When volatility is high, being 10% smarter or 10% bolder is an edge, but it requires teams to be daring, inclusive, and externally focused. For Deere, aligned means intentional conversations and multiple perspectives where the best questions and ideas can thrive. They ask, "What are our billion-dollar beliefs around digitalization, decarbonization, and industrial transitions?" "How

is the future going to be different from the past?" "What's the 'new' news?" "How easy is it to voice a divergent point of view or disagreement?" "Is counterfactual thinking a strength, and do we move beyond familiar sources of wisdom about our industry?" Discussing questions that force one to rethink first principles and embracing external and contrarian perspectives before making significant leadership commitments is always a good investment.

Aligning on the future growth story helps Deere's leaders separate the signal from the noise and is a foundation for team unity and trust. Leaders act with more courage and make decisions in a way that has concrete materiality and pace. Laser-focus around alignment, commitment, and execution happens through context-setting, choice-making, and direction-setting and helps keep the growth and value agenda on target.

2. **Need for speed:** Speed is a superpower. Deere knows they must move fast to be ready for a fast-changing world where competitive advantage is temporary, and you are either a disruptor or one of the disrupted. Leaders are now operating at the speed of AI, where high-velocity, high-quality decisions matter, and the agility to move in different directions is a given. It's playing offense (new paths to growth, partnerships, and investments) and defense (complexity reduction, cost reductions, and synergies across the firm). Hack Future Lab estimates a vast "need for speed" gap in most organizations, with 67% of leaders reporting barriers to moving faster.[12] One leader complained that she had sat through the same 30-minute presentation three times in separate meetings because no one had the authority to approve it.

   At Deere, leaders think of themselves as trustees of others' time. When we emphasize velocity without quality, the risk is missteps or worse. It is far better to maximize trust over control and power. For instance, pharma giant AstraZeneca uses a simplification drive to identify where value and talent are wasted.[13] The bottlenecks include too much manual paperwork, siloed meetings, and rules that slow the organizational speed clock. Hack Future Lab's research shows that universally, most employees don't believe that "decision-making is a strength in our firm" and "we are empowered to make decisions quickly."[14] The simplification drive, aptly called "The Million Hour Challenge," gives employees time to focus on higher-value work. AstraZeneca has saved more than 2 million hours so far, reinventing the time in drug discovery, and helped leaders fix the bottlenecks by adopting an outside-in view of the firm.[15]

Speed should not be used just for its own sake but with clear outcomes. Hack Future Lab's research shows that the adage "we can have good or fast decisions, but not both" is flawed. There is a strong correlation between fast decisions and good ones. At Deere, speedier learning and decision-making loops happen because leadership has evolved from Hippos (Highest Paid Person's Opinion) and hierarchy to trust and co-creation. A collaborative network of self-managing teams operates in rapid learning, doing, and reviewing cycles with zero compromises on the highest potential initiatives for creating value. That's intelligent speed.

3. **Return on courage:** The twentieth century organization chart, with hierarchy at its core, is on the ballot in an age of complexity and uncertainty. Leaders must build for courage, not for compliance, to meet new challenges, minimize risk, and open up new revenue streams. Deere embraces the return on courage principle through its connection to a higher purpose, strategic clarity, leadership alignment, and

focused action. Deere's bold transformation journey is a compelling example of a return on courage and a commitment to leadership in transitioning to a cleaner and more sustainable future. The firm's dedication to using fully autonomous tractors, agile supply chains, robots, drones, and carbon capture, utilization, and storage (CCUS) has made it a "courage pioneer." Since areas like power, industry, and transport are responsible for 70% of carbon emissions worldwide, Deere's leadership has boldly pivoted to the future, changing how it does things across its business and making courage its North Star.[16] It has intentionally chosen a path of proactive resilience.

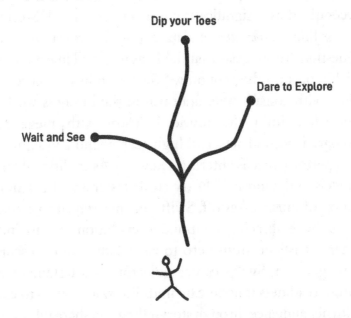

Return on courage is a mindset and skill set that helps everyone address the organizational upheavals around them and achieve sustained resilient performance: setting a bold growth agenda, the need for speed, and augmenting thinking through AI as a co-thinker. It's a new style of leadership that explicitly nurtures boldness as a cultural value, adopting bold behaviors as cultural norms, such as the courage to learn, the humility to unlearn, the clarity to focus, and the conviction to decide. Opportunity expands or shrinks in direct proportion to the return on daily courage. Taylor Swift, one of the biggest pop stars in the world, says, "Life isn't how to survive the storm; it's about how to dance in the rain."[17] She is authentically self-aware and in tune with the times, having already made an indelible mark on the music industry. She has emerged as the most streamed artist on both Apple Music and Spotify, establishing herself as one of the top-selling musicians ever. Her impact extends beyond music, as she has been recognized as a significant contributor to the US economy. According to *Fortune*, a data report by research company QuestionPro suggests that the Eras tour will inject more than $5 billion into the economy.[18] Swift's enduring success coincides with considerable upheaval in the business world, particularly within the music industry with mega arenas, hologram second acts, and high-tech sound and light shows; pop performance is entering a new era. As traditional business models in the music industry erode faster and the democratization of music takes off, Swift puts her return to courage to work by embracing continuous evolution. In an industry where artists go from hero to zero, fading into obscurity as time goes on, Swift's career trajectory is a testament to her future readiness muscle. She finds innovative ways to connect with her audience through storytelling and shareable moments of surprise unique to every show, ensuring that her work continues to resonate with her existing fans and new ones.

There is a mindset and cadence to getting things done. Swift leads from the future, embracing new AI-driven platforms and curating collective community moments to get closer to her fans. It's human connection and personalization at a hyper-scale. Whether you are a leader in a complex industrial firm like Deere or part of the AI revolution, we can all be inspired by Swift's courage to reinvent herself multiple times in the face of disruption, renewing her claim on the future and staying relevant in a courageous way.

Willful Contrarianism

It takes purposeful courage to play multiple positions in a game; the same is true in business. Leaders courageous enough to adopt willful contrarianism are likelier to see the future first and hone a courage edge that helps them take advantage of disruption and seize new growth opportunities. Willful contrarianism explicitly takes a point of view about the future that runs counter to conventional business wisdom and is a powerful antidote to the curse of sameness. Every firm thinks it's unique but, despite their best efforts, is more likely to be very similar to their industry peers. Take the investor buzz around Big Tech's financial gains despite every firm having the same "AI-everywhere" strategy or wanting to be "leaner and more efficient." With access to the same capabilities, most leaders suffer from leadership FOMO, playing a strategy game of imitation over innovation. The risk of sameness will likely worsen as AI adoption and the democratization of everything spreads, yet this differs from the courage advantage; leaders must evolve from a collective fear of change to embracing evolution at the speed of change itself.

If leaders ask, "What are we doing differently that our competition isn't?" what would you answer? I asked a team at a technology firm the same question, and their response was, "AI co-pilots." The problem was when I asked leaders at three other competitors the same question, the response was the same. Naturally, this has happened. Firms are essentially thinking about the future in the same way, constantly chasing the "shiny new thing." Remember the metaverse? Leaders must recognize sameness when it happens and explore the contrarian view to help break the spell and risk a race to the bottom. We will get the same outcome if we keep doing the same thing, especially with spiraling costs, inflation, and changing customer preferences.

Sameness around growth is a problem, too. Hack Future Lab's research shows that across all industries, leaders believe 60% of their revenues will come from new markets, products, or business models within the next five years. Yet, on average, every industry only achieves between 3% and 12% growth from new or adjacent breakout businesses.[19] The math doesn't work. Leaders are in denial about the sameness dilemma and its corrosive impact on future readiness. How much of our mindset is impacting our view of tomorrow? A mindset of courage sees the upside in disruption: choice, opportunity, and growth. A mindset of fear misses the upside of disruption. It reduces opportunity.

At Patagonia, willful contrarianism is part of its DNA. Founded in 1973 in California by rock climber Yvon Chouinard, it now boasts hundreds of outlets on five continents. Despite being well known for selling outdoor apparel, its origins are in climbing gear since climbing enthusiast Chouinard saw the need for tools that wouldn't harm rocks early on.[20] Since the 1980s, the firm's "1% for the Planet Scheme" has allocated 1% of its sales toward preserving and restoring the natural environment, resulting in $140 million in donations to support grassroots environmental groups worldwide.[21] We all know that the world is not in good shape, and signs of the extreme, and in some cases, irreversible changes humans have made to the climate are now impossible to ignore. The UN Secretary-General says that "our world is burning," and the Intergovernmental Panel on Climate

Change (IPCC) warns, "It is unequivocal that human influence has warmed the atmosphere, ocean, and land."[22]

Every industry is held captive to the sameness strategy: growth at any cost, value extraction, short-termism, and linear consumption patterns mean humanity's demand for nature exceeds what ecosystems can supply. According to a World Wildlife Fund (WWF) study, "more than a third of Earth's natural resources have been destroyed by humans in just 30 years," leading to an ecological overshoot and 60% of animals going extinct since the 1960s.[23] For Chouinard, climate risk isn't just a business risk. It's a force for willful contrarianism because a long-term sustainable future has no alternative. In an annual letter, Chouinard writes, "Even public companies with good intentions are under too much pressure to create short-term gain at the expense of long-term vitality and responsibility. There were no good options available. So, we created our own."[24] Chouinard, already one of the most provocative thinkers about capitalism's social purpose, has decided to raise the contrarianism stakes and make Earth his company's only shareholder.

Economist Milton Friedman's notion that a company's sole purpose is to maximize shareholder profits presupposed a world where entire industries are always one step ahead of the regulators.[25] The fashion industry dumps 2.1 billion tons of carbon dioxide into the atmosphere yearly. That's equal to the pollution from 456,707,817 cars in the same time frame, and globally, just 12% of the materials used for clothing end up recycled.[26] Chouinard's willful contrarianism has allowed him to reject Friedman's famous dictum because he doesn't believe the model of shareholder capitalism is good for the world. He doesn't even think it's good for capitalism.

In a letter about the decision, published on the Patagonia website, he writes of "reimagining capitalism," moving from empty platitudes about sustainability to anchoring purpose in unwavering values. The Patagonia Purpose Trust and the Holdfast Collective, a group of non-profit organizations, will now own the privately held firm's stock and channel the profits to environmental causes. It expects to give $100 million annually to support causes that repair, restore, and regenerate our world and make great companies. "Instead of extracting value from nature and transforming it into wealth for investors, we'll use the wealth Patagonia creates to protect the source of all wealth," he says. "Each year, the money we make after reinvesting in the business will be distributed as a dividend to help fight the crisis." Chouinard's willful contrarianism has enabled Patagonia to replace timidity with boldness; it has rejected the external pressure to deliver "more with less" and comes when business needs more contrarian leaders. It could be said that Patagonia made the ultimate bold pivot to a circular future; instead of going "public," they are going all in on "purpose."[27]

Here are three lessons for any leader to unlock the benefits of willful contrarianism and a contrarian mindset.

1. Start with billion-dollar beliefs

A billion-dollar belief is thinking on a different horizon and answering "What are we certain about?" with clear-eyed conviction. Billion-dollar beliefs give leaders a determined focus on what matters and are clarifiers for bringing a bold leadership agenda to life. Sustainability is a here-to-stay billion-dollar belief that is more than moving away from being something you do to have a little green label to increasingly putting your whole business model, strategy, and value chain in a much more resilient position. It's about making products nature-positive and reversing nature loss, but it's also about multiplying value for a better tomorrow. Too many leaders disempower themselves by constantly chasing uncertainty. Don't be an "uncertainty chaser." A wiser and less common approach is to frame the future with the certainties of a billion-dollar belief.

2. Avoid the "tragedy of the horizon"

How do long-term-focused leaders thrive in a short-term world? I was invited to speak about leading in the future alongside Mark Carney, the former governor of the Bank of England. A big takeaway from our conversation was the "tragedy of the horizon" – a collective blind spot where many leaders linger. Most business cycles are short-term, whether quarterly earning reports, annual performance reviews, or central bank forecasts. Leaders become "nowists" under pressure to prioritize short-term results and strategies of sameness over long-term thinking. Patagonia takes a deeper strategic perspective by pulling future challenges, such as climate risk, back to the present to make the right bold but necessary decisions today. Leaders are more willing to make more significant, more courageous decisions when they lead from the future instead of the present. That's how we solve the tragedy of the horizon.[28]

3. In bold, we thrive

The days of focusing solely on the shareholder are gone. Firms anchoring their strategies to a meaningful purpose, focusing on creating long-term sustainable value, will win. Tackling climate risk is not just improving supply chains or offsetting carbon emissions. For Patagonia, it demands rethinking, re-focusing, and re-positioning the DNA of what the firm does, why it does it, and how it does it. Adopting billion-dollar beliefs will cause some industries to shrink and others to expand. Patagonia has turned its billion-dollar beliefs of responsible business and stakeholder capitalism that respects nature into a platform for future readiness: it shows the urgency to move away from economist Milton Friedman's narrow definition of capitalism, encouraging leaders to look for better ways to reconcile capitalism and the climate crisis. The takeaway is that making a business sustainable and profitable is not mutually exclusive. Solving the "tragedy of the horizon" amid intensifying environmental and waste challenges is possible. By seizing the upside of rethinking cycles and embracing change before it becomes an existential risk, Patagonia is an organization already living in the future.

The Mindset Advantage

How much of your mindset is impacting your leadership choices? The twin super cycles of geopolitical risk and AI compete for leaders' attention in ways that make us feel anxious or powerless about the future. Now more than ever, a leader's mindset must be able to separate "headline risk" from noise. The World Uncertainty Index is a measure that tracks uncertainty across the world by text-mining the country reports of the Economist Intelligence Unit. According to its latest index, uncertainty is at record levels driven by geopolitical tensions in the Middle East and Ukraine, the outcome of the US election, the US-China relationship, and macro topics such as growth, inflation, and monetary and fiscal policies.[29] Yet, the future has always been uncertain and volatile. Stanford Professor Scott Sagan once said something that every leader should hang on their wall: "Things that have never happened before happen all the time."[30] History is mostly a series of multiplying and overlapping disruptions: war and genocide, to disaster and disease, from terrorism to election violence and economic collapse.

The history of leadership is a history of unpredictable shocks upon shocks in all forms over the last hundred years. Today's disruptions, from the dot com crises and global financial crisis to the global pandemic and the war in Ukraine, demand leaders to respond intelligently and boldly. Perhaps it's time for leaders to stop chasing uncertainty and embrace disruption as the norm and as a tailwind for decisive action. Many have dubbed this new world "Perma Crises or Poly Crises," a new operating reality where productivity, technology enablement, and sustainability drive future success and leadership courage is the fuel.[31]

How will the AI and decarbonization revolution play out? Will our leadership withstand the next crisis? How do we make megatrends our business and capitalize on the disruptive forces of the last few years to create a future with intentionality? There is no courage without vulnerability. One of the most courageous actions a leader can take is to be brave enough to "know that you don't know everything" and that it's okay. It's leadership through listening, seeing, feeling, and being, not just "knowing." Clayton Christensen, the academic and author of *The Innovator's Dilemma: When New Technologies Cause Great Firms to Fail*, had a wooden sign on his office door that said, "Anomalies Welcome."[32] In most office settings, signs display our names, job titles, or departments. However, Christensen's sign served a greater purpose.

It symbolized his invitation to embrace challenges and upend assumptions. Anomalies are weak signals that are unseen or surprising but not fully understood. Many leaders overlook them because they don't fit into existing patterns, yet anomalies can help us see around corners with a glimpse of what could be.

The founders of Instagram initially developed a social networking app named Burbn. However, they quickly noticed significant user engagement with the image-sharing feature. This made them rethink their initial approach, a "false start." Through the anomaly, they realized the app's true purpose was photo sharing. Christensen understood that progress and learning arise from exploring the unknown and that a dose of volatility can limit overconfidence.[33]

Beyond being a hand-carved wooden sign on Christensen's door at Harvard Business School, the "Anomalies Welcome" sign symbolizes something more extraordinary. It invites us to connect with new worlds, sparking fresh perspectives and unlocking a world of possibility. Courage and humility are inseparable.

The Beyonders

Is your organization a beyonder? The term beyonder was coined by psychologist Ellis Paul Torrance, who described it as "going beyond where you've never been before and beyond where others have been before."[34] A beyonder organization outpaces its industry peers and performs *beyond* expectations consistently. It's defined as high execution certainty (we know our priorities) and high trust certainty (we trust each other). Beyonders are the opposite of preservers of the status quo: They learn aggressively, adopt "disrupt and grow" mindsets, and are relentlessly truthful about what gives them an "edge."

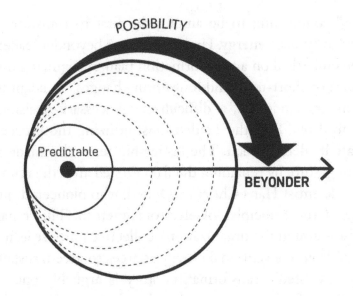

Ørsted, the Danish energy firm formerly known as DONG Energy, has emerged as a beyonder in the global transition toward renewable energy. Ørsted has undergone a remarkable reinvention, transforming from a traditional fossil fuel firm into a worldwide leader in offshore wind energy and sustainable practices. In its early years, Ørsted, like many conventional energy companies, primarily relied on fossil fuels for energy generation. However, in the early 2000s, it faced growing challenges and uncertainties related to environmental concerns, climate change, and the global shift toward cleaner energy sources. A pivotal moment in Ørsted's beyonder journey started when the firm faced a crisis – a downgrade in its credit rating to negative, which resulted in increased debt costs and an adapt-or-die moment in its history.[35]

In response, the board appointed Henrik Poulsen, a former leader known for his vision and strategic courage at LEGO, as the new CEO. Where many leaders might have resorted to crisis management tactics, such as large-scale layoffs, Poulsen and his team recognized this as an opportunity for "going beyond where you've never been before and beyond where others have been before," committing to be among the first to transition from "black" to "green" energy. Under Poulsen's beyonder leadership, Ørsted embarked on a transformation plan, recognizing the significance of short-term and long-term changes. To adapt to the new energy landscape, a difficult but necessary decision was made to divest 8 of the 12 divisions, utilizing the proceeds to alleviate its debt burden. The leadership team also made a significant gesture by renaming the firm Ørsted after the renowned Danish scientist Hans Christian Ørsted, who pioneered the discovery of the principles of electromagnetism. This renaming exercise elevated the organization's collective purpose as it transitioned from conventional energy sources to green, sustainable energy.[36] Ørsted's transformation story is arguably one of the boldest transformations in the last decade for a complex, legacy firm. Previously, with 80% ownership by the Danish government, Ørsted's IPO became one of Denmark's most significant, a testament to investors' confidence in its strategic direction. Notably, net profits have surged by more than $5 billion since its IPO, underscoring the resilience of the reinvention. Today, Ørsted stands tall as the world's largest offshore wind operator with a market cap of more than $20 billion, boasting an impressive 30% share of the rapidly expanding global offshore wind energy market.[37]

At the heart of Ørsted's reinvention lies beyonder leadership, turning megatrends such as the energy transition into global renewables into concrete milestones. Recognizing the critical need for a radical shift toward renewable energy, divesting from declining sectors, and aggressively pursuing cost reductions in offshore wind power, Ørsted has secured its future and emerged as a global leader in decarbonization. The journey to "go beyond where you've never been before and beyond where others have been before" starts with adopting a beyonder mindset of risk-taking and resilience. Exploring a series of mindset-shifting questions can help ignite a beyonder movement in your organization.

1. **Radical receptivity:** When considering our business's core strengths and challenges, what will happen over the next five years, and what would an activist investor do in our shoes?

2. **Reimagine growth pathways:** Given the above risks, inflection points, and challenges, what new business models, products, and services should we commit to and why?

3. **Leadership:** What are the new leadership mindsets and reframing for turning volatility into value creation and strategic courage to move fast and make the impossible possible?

Ørsted's remarkable journey from a negative credit rating to becoming the world's leading offshore wind farm operator offers three powerful lessons in beyonder leadership, grit, and sustainable business practices.

1. **Turn megatrends into milestones:** Beyonders are skilled at making the "trend their friend." Ørsted's strategic pivot to leading from the future began by recognizing that the energy transition to global renewables is a here-to-stay secular trend that is more than moving away from being something you do to have a little green label to increasingly putting your whole business model, strategy, and value chain in a much more resilient and future-ready position. By making bold moves early around the future growth story and embracing disruption as a calling for reinvention, Ørsted leaped ahead of its industry peers and is well placed to multiply value for the next hundred years. Leaders who make megatrends their business and prioritize long-term horizons over short ones will be the ones who lead the future.

2. **Forever beta:** If you were starting as leaders again today, what mindsets would you keep, and which ones would you eliminate? An unmistakable sign of beyonder leadership is rethinking assumptions and updating mindsets in cycles. Ørsted didn't blindly scale back its ambitions in the face of a crisis. Instead, they recognized they could unlock the enormous growth potential of the global transition to renewable energy and scale new capabilities faster than their competitors. Beyonders are outward-looking and have an aligned viewpoint on the future while allowing for wriggle room to respond to emerging signals. They showed anticipation skills to see the emerging opportunity of decarbonization, acted on it, and harnessed enterprise-wide courage skills to assimilate new ideas from other industries and turn risk into the upside. Leading in a forever beta world of change everywhere reminds us we always have a choice: we can be leaders, followers, or out-of-business.

3. **Beyonder cultures:** Culture is like pouring concrete. It can take a while to set, but changing afterward is much more challenging. A beyonder culture, such as Ørsted's, develops and rewards courage skills. For instance, there are OKRs for courage over conformity and speaking up over silence to avoid empty slogans and leadership buzzwords that afflict our organizations. Hack Future Lab took the pulse of 300 business leaders globally. An overwhelming 91% agreed that culture is critical for business success. The bad news was that more than half the group reported that a beyonder culture was not an existing strength and that "it's too easy to pay lip service to organizational culture."[38] Most leaders see culture as incredibly important but mismanaged and undervalued. At Ørsted, they committed to a culture where the courage advantage is the heart of everything they do.

Wanted – Leaders of Courage

We need to face facts. You can't lead from the future without daily courage. The courage to take risks, the courage to think big, the courage to say "no" and eliminate the unnecessary. The current paradigm of leaders as preservers of the status quo must be reimagined as leaders of courage skills. We have cultures that reward bureaucratic work and compliance-led KPIs more than intelligent work. This is insanity. Only then will organizations be able to turn the AI and skills revolution into a tailwind for new learning, growth, and meaningful work.

The courage advantage is a wake-up call from the future and demands leaders to be "yes, and" not "yes, but" people. I've grown up in a "yes, but" world defined by risk-avoiding mindsets and a shared fear of change or adapting to anything new. We desperately need a post-AI model of leadership, talent, and culture fit for the Intelligence Age, and arguably, that will be one of the most significant upsides of disruption for those daring enough to grab it. It's a "yes, and" future.

Takeaways

- **Adopt a contrarian mindset:** The future is not a fact. It's the sum total of mindsets, decisions, and actions. How do we seize the future boldly? It starts and ends with courage, the most important of virtues. Courage should not mean chasing headlines or virtue signaling from leaders who want to be seen as ethical or concerned about talent, data privacy, and job automation. Fake do-goodery can easily backfire. We've seen the hypocrisy of some firms claiming to be responsible and ethical organizations when they're chasing profits at the expense of safety or global emissions. The more courageous we claim to be, the more scrutiny we are likely to attract, but that should not put us off because today's challenges can't be solved with Industrial Age thinking and status quo–preserving mindsets.

Patagonia's willful contrarianism to make Earth its only shareholder allowed it to break free from the curse of the sameness strategy that's in every firm's playbook: growth at any cost, zero-sum value extraction, and short-termism over long-term planning. It showed that climate risk is more than just investor risk: It's a force for purpose-led leadership, new learning curves, and the flexibility to avoid getting trapped in the "tragedy of the horizon" and missing the future when it arrives.

A contrarian mindset replaces fear with action. The easiest thing a leader can do is "wait and see." Perhaps we decide to "dip our toes in" and test the waters, but today's operating environment of hyper-speed and hyper-change means a leader's rethinking cycle is required much faster. Chouinard's contrarian mindset rejected the external pressure to deliver "more with less" and showed it's possible to lead for today and tomorrow's world. It chose to create its destiny.

- **Put billion-dollar beliefs to work:** It's impossible to seize the future without decisively putting our billion-dollar beliefs to work. Billion-dollar beliefs are significant forces that shape the world and disrupt entire industries but also, more immediately, can unlock enormous upside and give leaders a unique chance to reimagine a bolder future. Decarbonization is one of the most influential billion-dollar beliefs. Yet, many organizations still view it as an operational threat rather than a pivotal moment to rethink what it means to be a profitable and sustainable business. For Ørsted, its billion-dollar belief was thinking on a different timescale and answering, "What are we certain about?"

Billion-dollar beliefs help leaders decide what matters and are clarifiers for bringing a new strategy to life. Too many leaders disempower themselves by constantly obsessing about uncertainty. Don't chase uncertainty. It drains us of the resources and agility to think differently about the future. As my friend Professor Dave Ulrich says, "Replace uncertainty you cannot control with certainty you can." A wiser and less common approach is to frame the future with beliefs and certainties that you can invest with time, energy, and talent. The question "What's *not* going to change?" rarely gets asked, yet it's the one question that can help leaders focus on what matters.

The leadership at Ørsted showed the courage to acknowledge that, like most firms today, they are organized for a rapidly disappearing world – an era of "profit maximization at any costs," and it will be billion-dollar beliefs such as digitalization, ethical impact, and decarbonization which overwrite that.

Is it possible to make sustainability sustainable? Ørsted has answered the question: it made a strategic pivot to the future by putting its billion-dollar beliefs to work into the energy transition to global renewables.

- **Sharpen courage skills:** Leaders can use different courage practices to strengthen their mindset in challenging times: take a break to speed up progress (step back from the challenge to find a solution); embrace your lack of knowledge (listen without assumptions); boldly change the way you ask questions (pose challenging questions to challenge your mental model); set direction, not just a destination (lead with a context, not just goals); and test your solutions, and yourself (conduct experiments that allow for failure to generate breakthrough ideas).

Overthinking is a big problem in most organizations, creating risk aversion, bureaucracy, and bottlenecks that become obstacles to courage. Future anxiety is one of the most significant types of overthinking, with the acceleration of AI as a potential disruptor of jobs and security. Waiting for complete uncertainty is a losing strategy in an era of perpetual risk and upheaval. Without sharpening our courage skills, we can't lean into the future, navigate tech disruption, or turn volatility into value creation.

It's impossible to out-pace the forces of disruption or achieve a high return on insights or intelligence if our organizations comprise sameness and conformists. Great ideas happen when people can bring their divergence to the job (BYOD). How would your teams rate their return on courage within the organization? Is it exceeding or behind expectations? I partnered with a technology client (let's call it Zeta Technology) that wanted to sharpen its courage and cognitive skills for an emerging world of new competitors, new customers, and new ways of working by introducing Courage Skills Month. More than 30,000 employees worldwide can access virtual and in-person "courage tracks" on themes such as BE the Change and Get Future-fit. The outcome is that participants can curate their courage journey to become courageous doers. It's courage at the human scale.

- **Go beyond:** Fluidity and fearlessness are essential leadership instincts in playing multiple positions in a game, just as they are in business. We live in an era of risk and uncertainties. As old barriers to entry fall and the only competitive advantage is today, the most successful leaders are beyonders, balancing prudence in risk management with a relentless pursuit of the upside. A solely defensive approach tends to result in average results and performance, while an offense-only stance may bring occasional wins and significant failures.

Leaders who dare to evolve and pursue both strategies simultaneously will create enduring advantages over the long term. John Deere's bold move into automating its tractors and allocating intelligent investments in precision ag technology, robotic bees, and drones show beyonder's urgency for radical innovation, agility, and opportunism amidst industry disruption and changing customer preferences.

Beyonders thrive despite volatility, whether it's Microsoft reinventing itself as an AI-first pioneer or music artist Taylor Swift's capacity to embrace new platforms of expression with surprise and creativity. Just as a system upgrade revitalizes software, beyonders harness culture as a catalyst to upend lazy assumptions about the future and achieve sustained success. They align values like courage, trust, and collaboration with what the future needs, treating culture like a product, constantly iterating it so that employee value propositions are alive visibly and humans go beyond their highest potential.

- **Don't go it alone:** Courage depends on the strength of our relationships, and great ideas happen when people can bring their divergence to the job (BYOD). It takes diverse connections and influencing skills to overcome practical leadership challenges, from replacing "checking" with continuous coaching and "transactional" conversations with "transformational" ones. As David Bohn said, "Real dialogue is where two or more people become willing to suspend their certainty in each other's presence."[39] Energy multiplies when people with a shared purpose unite to do something meaningful and make a difference. We should be truthful about what gives us energy in our daily work and look under the hood as a team. When there are more courageous moments, results are easier to come by, and we begin to trust each other more, which is the starting point for a thriving and happier team.

Spy novelist John le Carre wrote, "A desk is a dangerous place from which to view the world."[40] To avoid going alone, invest time and trust in humans, not just technology. When was the last time you learned something about someone else or embraced or helped others overcome their challenges? A missing link for leaders to be alert to is that the more senior our role is, the greater the risk that we will be protected from bad news and issues about performance. It shouldn't be that way and can be a sign of a culture of fear and conformity, the ultimate speak-up destroyer. Make ecosystems of trust a priority because that's the best way to unlock the remarkable untapped potential of our people and see them flourish. We don't just want to go to work; we want to learn, grow, and belong. Muditā is a Sanskrit word for taking joy in other people's success and well-being and is a cornerstone of any leader who, as designer Thomas Heatherwick observed, needs nutritional value and isn't just "knowing" but listens, connects, and sees. It's humans learning, thriving, and growing together.[41]

Evolution: In Trust, We Grow

"Trust is risky. It's vulnerable. It's a leap of faith. . . . The more we trust, the farther we can venture."

– Esther Perel

Every Christmas, I visit the European city of Ljubljana, charmingly known as the city of dragons, to join my partner's family for a well-earned vacation. Ljubljana is a city of medieval castles, pastel-colored buildings, and medieval market squares. With winter temperatures dropping below zero degrees, I eat and drink more than I should, especially hot chocolate, hearty "Jota" soups, and a delicious local cake called "Potica." One late afternoon, after exploring local bookshops and galleries, my partner and I discovered a small coffee shop in Ljubljana's downtown district. Each table was adorned with candle sticks, and the lighting was just right, so we settled there for a few hours, talking and sipping hot coffees. The next day, I realized I had left my new scarf in the coffee shop and said to my partner, "There is no way the scarf will still be there now." We decided to find out either way and returned to the coffee shop where, surprised, I discovered my scarf neatly folded and exactly where I had left it.

Wearing my scarf again, I thought about why trust is the ultimate currency for leaders to navigate the future and trust certainty gives others the clarity to turn talk into action.

TRUST CERTAINTY

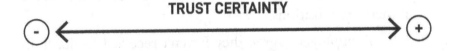

Without trust, leadership breaks down, companies go bust, and cultures decay. How do we sustain trust in our organizations during record levels of distrust, global fracturing, and AI-driven misinformation? Is it time to rethink the importance of trust in scaling a human-led, AI-enabled future?

Truth Decay in Organizations

A collision of trust, politics, and leadership has led to a record decline of trust in our leadership and institutions, from the media and government to non-government organizations and businesses. According to Edelman's annual trust barometer, businesses still lead on trust, but it scores below 60%, while the media is actively distrusted.[1] Without trust, culture breaks down, customers lose interest, and talent walks out of the door. A cursory look at the WEF Davos agenda over the last few years reveals the red lights flashing on the leadership and trust dashboard. Themes such as "Restoring Trust," "The Future of Trust," and "Trust in AI" are common. And while I frequently see moonshots for technology, I rarely see a moonshot for trust.[2]

This matters because leaders are losing the trust of their stakeholders worldwide, which has dire consequences for steering their organizations through accelerating and multiplying technology, economic, and geopolitical disruption.

Trust on the Ballot

- 73% of employees are worried that AI could take their jobs in the next five years
- 54% of employees agree that trust is not a core "living" value in their organizations
- 53% of employees agree they haven't received feedback in the last three months
- 36% of employees trust their organization's leadership to do the right thing
- 28% of employees would trust a stranger more than a boss

Source: Hack Future Lab

Trust in Humans

Within every organization, leaders must ask, "How do we get the best from our people?" Trust is the answer. Trust is a leap of faith into the unknown and is the cornerstone of every high-performing leader and organization. Financial trust. Digital trust. Ethical trust. Leadership trust. When trust outcomes are high, cost and time go *down*, and speed goes up; likewise, when trust outcomes are low, cost and time go up, and speed goes down. There's a strong correlation between trust and smart risk-taking: if we feel trusted, we're more inclined to take courageous leaps into the future when navigating difficult-to-predict scenarios.

Here are four reasons trust is the currency of humans and at the core of searching and finding the upside of disruption.

- **Trust is a clarifier:** Low levels of trust across the organization can cause fragmented alignment, misunderstandings, and fear. Most leadership problems come down to one word: clarity. Hack Future Lab's research on trust in leaders shows that only 27% of employees agree that their leaders communicate clearly how changes made today will impact their organization. Just 4 in 10 are fully aligned around the top must-win priorities. Leaders consistently overestimate the level of alignment and commitment in their teams and fail to clarify issues and concerns before they become emergencies because they are drowning in meetings, information, and technology that make the urgent seem important.[3] Leaders must relentlessly communicate and reinforce clarity to separate the signal from the noise and ensure high execution certainty and trust around the top strategic priorities.

- **Trust is a simplifier:** Success creates complexity, and complexity kills success. It's easier for leaders to reduce complexity with simplicity when trust is high because messages travel faster across the organization in high-trust operating contexts, and teams feel accountable for their results. Barriers to working with greater clarity and efficiency undermine talent and derail performance. Hack Future Lab's research shows that 67% of leaders agree that "complexity is a barrier to agility"; only 41% can link value to the enterprise and align their resources to their biggest priorities. When trust is high, decisions are faster, more fluid, and more effective.[4]

- **Trust is an energizer:** COVID-19 and hybrid working brought trust and employee well-being to the forefront, and it will continue to dominate leadership conversations in the years to come. The bad news is that two-thirds of employees are suffering record burnout and overwork today. There is even a new word to describe the worldwide human energy crisis: Meta-anxiety, which means anxiety about "anxiety." Without trust, there's no energy; without energy, there's no commitment and no innovation. Hack Future Lab's research shows that employees' willingness to absorb enterprise-wide transformation has dropped from 63% to 47% in the last 18 months, and only 33% of leaders have complete confidence in their teams' output levels.[5] As HR thinker Josh Bersin says: "People are overworked. 81% of them are burned out, and 87% are overworked. We've got to re-engineer how we get to this new business model and bring the people with us."[6]

- **Trust gives you a "no" strategy:** How do we get laser-like focus on our leadership priorities? It starts with having a "no" strategy because strategy is about tough choices and what not to do. Trust certainty means "we are fully aligned and committed to the direction." When trust certainty is high, ideas travel faster, and friction (time, cost, issues) reduces. When trust certainty is low, ideas travel slower, and friction (time, cost, issues) increases. Hack Future Lab's research shows that 73% of leaders agree that there are too many conflicting strategic priorities and commitments to focus on what matters.[7] A "no" strategy is one of the best forms of optimization because it demands we stop wasting time on activities that don't support the strategy. It helps leaders stay nimble and focused on growth as their organization scales and ensures boundaries are respected. CVS, the global health provider, pivoted to a healthier future in line with its customers' evolving needs by deciding that its "no" strategy was to end the sale of tobacco products. Making the call to forego more than $2 billion in annual sales from cigarette and tobacco products became straightforward once the leadership team aligned around a shared view of the future, decided the boundaries, and worked backward from there.[8] A "no" strategy gives others the trust and certainty to own their decisions.

Trust Decay

Who can you trust? An exchange of trust defines every leadership action and interaction, and yet, at no time has trust been more tested by customers, employees, and each other. Leadership is facing its moment of truth. George Orwell, best known for his novels *Animal Farm* and *Nineteen Eighty-Four*, would have relished these times. Fake news, false facts, ethical fading, meme warfare, data breaches, tainted food, and digital skulduggery. It's not our imagination. More companies are operating at the edge of ethics in pursuing profits, and trust and transparency are under scrutiny by regulators, media, talent, and customers.

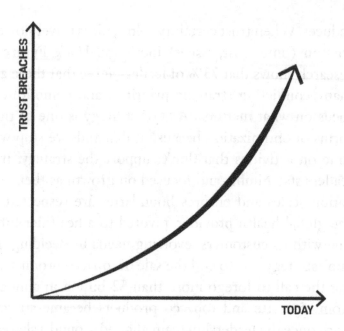

Leaders who want to win with trust must lead on trust, earning and building it daily. Trust and accountability follow when the present is clearly defined, and employees feel inspired and set up for success when the future is championed. The relentless demands of leading in a world of hyper-scale and hyper-speed mean that leaders have an institutional bias to "move fast and break things" rather than "slow down and fix things." The commercial and human implications of trust and ethical breaches are significant, with the impact on businesses alone estimated to cost organizations billions of dollars globally in lost productivity.[9] Humans lose faith in their leaders to do the right thing and become more anxious about losing their jobs to AI, robots, and algorithms.

According to Hack Future Lab estimates, 10 out of 15 industry sectors have reported a collapse in trust over the last three years, and there are plenty of examples for leaders to study:

- Sam Bankman Fried, the CEO of cryptocurrency exchange FTX, one of the world's largest cryptocurrency exchanges with a market cap of $32 billion, was found guilty of fraud and stealing as much as $10 billion in customer money.

- Trevor Milton, the CEO of Nikola, a pioneering electric and hydrogen-powered truck maker, was convicted of fraud and misleading investors about the firm's technical achievements to secure more funding.

- Elizabeth Holmes, the founder of Theranos Inc., a biotech startup, is serving a long sentence for fraud and false claims to regulators and investors about faulty technology that tested people's blood.

- The collapse of Wirecard, a German payment processing innovator and once Europe's most valued fintech at €24 billion, for corrupt business practices and fraudulent financial reporting. One executive is thought to still be on the run.

- The British Post Office scandal, a state-owned entity that presided over a culture of secrecy and intimidation, saw more than 700 "sub-postmasters" prosecuted for theft and false accounting when shortfalls in money were, in fact, due to errors of the Post Office's flagship Horizon Accounting Software.

As talent scarcity increases, trust is a source of future readiness. Yet, many companies forget to do the basics brilliantly, starting with trust. Leaders have a "trust" problem. See how groupthink, willful blindness, secrecy, and an inability to connect the dots have been standard features for every organization that has suffered a major trust breach. Without trust, there's no accountability. It's hubris over humility – the opposite of trust-focused leadership. It's time for leaders to reassess how they bake trust into their leadership, strategy, and purpose and use it as their North Star for a more humane and trust-led future.

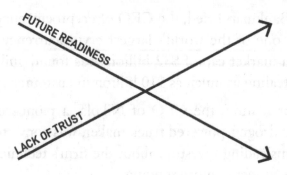

The Trust Mindset

Trust was historically considered a "soft" leadership issue. Its connection to a firm's value was always there but unclear. Betrayals of trust have major financial consequences. *The Economist* studied eight of the largest recent business scandals, comparing the firms involved with their peer groups, and found they had forfeited significant amounts of value. The median firm was worth 30% less than it would have been valued had it not experienced a scandal.[10] Trust can't afford to be an afterthought for leaders because people are more likely to embrace transformation, take ownership, and make things happen if there is trust in our leaders and each other. Research by Statista shows that by 2025, global digital transformation spending will reach $5.9 trillion.[11] Yet, countless hours of time, effort, and billions of dollars are wasted annually on failed transformations because of a lack of trust.

As leaders try to crack the code to scale ecosystems of trust and higher productivity levels, Hack Future Lab has found that when leaders activate a Trust Mindset, most employees agree that they feel "empowered and trusted to co-create the future together" and are three times more likely to believe "that resilience is a strength in our organization." The Trust Mindset enables leaders to strengthen three trust dimensions: (1) Who we are (identity), (2) How we work (agility), and (3) How we grow (scalability). By harnessing the three trust dimensions early, leaders are 2.1X more likely to outperform their industry peers, 4.7X more likely to be described as "great places to work," and 5.6X more likely to be innovative because trust and innovation are two sides of the same coin.[12]

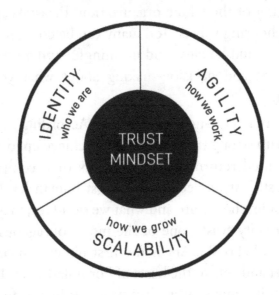

1. Who We Are (Identity)

How do we get real gut-level buy-in to the future growth story? It starts with boldly and definitively declaring who we are (value of values) and why we do what we do (shared purpose), which is the first dimension of the Trust Mindset. It's what academic Fobazi Ettarh calls "vocational awe" – a collective sense of mission-driven community.[13] Answering the "Who We Are" question helps leaders avoid wanting to do everything and please everyone. The pandemic accelerated many things, including e-commerce, remote work, and a reawakening for people about the nature of work, why we work, and how we work.

Hack Future Lab's research shows that one-third of people are in continuous job search mode, and half are rethinking their careers. Having a shared purpose and identity about who we are helps us feel connected and wiser than the sum of our parts. It taps into the collective intelligence and belonging of the whole organization. Please keep it simple when choosing values: Too many can be counterproductive. Values should be clear and meaningful and guide mindsets, behaviors, and decision-making about what you are and are not.[14]

There is a financial impact, too: According to McKinsey, firms with strong trust-led cultures achieve up to three times higher total returns to shareholders than companies with low trust.[15] At its deepest and most human level, when we tell people who we are and what we stand for, they listen: it's "authenticity trust," one of the most courageous steps you can take. Who We Are is the first dimension of the Trust Mindset and cuts to the heart of Formula 1 (F1). This hyper-competitive industry is already living in the future, using more than 300 sensors on its racing cars to calculate 1.1 million data points per second. A gear change is 50X faster than the blink of an eye, and every season, more than 1 million parts are manufactured, and 30k design changes are made to adapt to different races.[16] The drivers must test the limits of human, cognitive, and technical excellence, and teams win with trust. F1 reminds leaders that every organization must sharpen the Who We Are question or risk losing relevancy.

Here's why:

- Like organizations, the F1 teams and their drivers operate in ecosystems of trust and excellence, showing trust in tech and trust in each other to win under extreme pressure.

- Like business models and cultures, racing cars must embrace a perpetual state of beta, learning, unlearning, and relearning to stay ahead of the competition.

- The F1 teams must learn at the speed of technology, and organizations must learn at the speed of the customer or risk falling behind.

- The F1 teams work alongside AI as co-pilots to elevate what makes them elite sportspeople, and organizations work with AI as co-thinkers to sharpen agility and speed to insights.

- Finally, every F1 team wants to win the future with teamwork, values, and trust. F1 teams articulate their values in actionable ways and understand the power of values in *action*.

One of the most unmistakable signs of the Trust Mindset in F1 is instinctively being connected and authentic about who they are. They obsess over values, not just metrics, and bind trust to freedom and accountability. Values inform decision-making, helping teams choose between competing priorities and reaffirm what the organization will give up to uphold those values. Who We Are is about making the invisible visceral, asking whether we humanize or commodify trust and purpose and whether we are empowered in our daily work. Who We Are matters for everyone, but especially the "Anxious Generation": those who are suffering record levels of automation anxiety (will AI take my job?) and future anxiety (will there be another pandemic or global conflict?). Designer Charles Eames said, "Eventually, everything connects."[17] Building the Who We Are dimension can sound like an abstract idea. F1 brings the Who We Are dimension to life by making the invisible visceral: Believing, Belonging, Braving, and Becoming.

Believing

The only real difference between one organization and another is the trust in its people and belief in the vision. In F1, believing in the mission, elevating purpose, and trusting each other to do the right thing are non-negotiable. Can team members connect their work to the future growth story and believe it makes a difference? What's clear is that people desire to work in believing cultures where trust is a source code for meaning, energy, and pride. Team rituals, recognition, and gatherings are not to be smirked at but instead harnessed as concrete ways to strengthen believing and a galvanizing sense of "we, not me." When we believe in our work and love what we do or at least part of it, we are less likely to suffer from burnout (cognitive and emotional burnout) or "bore out" (i.e., cognitive underload).

Belonging

Think of a time in your life when you felt productive and focused, and chances are belonging was a part of the experience. The need to belong is hardwired into our primal selves and is at the core of what makes us human. In F1, belonging means caring about each other for the benefit of the whole group. It demands generosity and honesty, sometimes patience, calling out issues, or giving tough but necessary feedback. Hack Future Lab's research shows that care and belonging are the new currency of work and a significant driver of equity, excellence, and trust. We're not a team because we work together. We're a team because we trust and believe in each other. Individuals who agree that "belonging is a strength in my team" are 4X more likely to describe themselves as "optimistic about the future" and 3X less likely to quit.[18] In a recent fireside chat with Professor Lynda Gratton, we discussed why nearly 300 million people report having no friends and why belonging and its cousin, social capital, is declining in many organizations. In an age of atomized work schedules, hybrid jobs, and endless meetings, 40% of the global labor force report feeling lonely sometimes. This should be a wake-up call to leaders everywhere.[19]

Braving

Success in F1 means braving. It's the daily courage to do the right thing, not the easy thing, and bring our vulnerabilities into full view. It's the courage to speak up, the courage to say "no," and the courage to give tough but must-be-heard feedback. Hack Future Lab's research reveals that one-third of the global labor force defaults to fear every month.[20] Try this experiment. Can you think of a recent time when you had something important to say in a meeting but held back because of fear? Chances are the answer is "yes." Most of us can think of a time when we didn't speak up because of fear, and it's even more taboo to speak up when the business is under pressure. The problem is that silence becomes the norm without a culture of braving. We lose an early warning system when people don't feel confident to speak up. Ideas are lost, and trust and talent are undermined.

Worse, minor problems become crises without the silence breakers and courageous doers. For F1 teams, everyone has a duty of care to bring braving to life in a visible way by asking two compelling questions:

1. What's not being said right now that should be said?
2. What would help us work with greater clarity and courage every day?

Make braving part of your everyday leadership so that it becomes a drumbeat for choosing courage over comfort zones and build a culture where it becomes taboo to *avoid* speaking up.

Becoming

F1 competes by the principle that innovation starts as an act of courage, but to sustain vitality requires imagination, the human force that can push through inertia. Organizations go from hero to zero 3X faster than a decade ago.[21] Your competitive advantage can best be described as "temporary" in a world where cross-industry competitors are rising and industry convergence is accelerating. Becoming is the answer to zombie leadership, which is the destiny of every organization if they ignore it. As leaders, it's our job to help identify hidden potential and challenge our limits. In F1, work performance is framed around learning goals, teamwork, and collective impact. Becoming is sustained by asking questions such as "How are we learning for tomorrow's world?" We are either adopting a spirit of perpetual beta, performing for today while growing for tomorrow, or we are at risk of doing what we've always done until it's too late to change.

Who We Are Is What We Do

Who We Are is the first dimension of the Trust Mindset, a multiplier for untapped energy, focus, and human connection. As machines get better at being machines, humans must get better at being humans. This doesn't mean toxic positivity. When times are tough, simply telling people to be positive does not strengthen their ability to overcome adversity. It fails to acknowledge the anxieties they are going through. Leaders must elevate what makes us more human, avoiding artificial interactions at all costs, from fake empowerment to cringeworthy "feedback sandwiches." They are trust destroyers and a fast track to disengaged employees who have mentally quit the job but continue to turn up like shadows of their former selves. Strengthening the Who We Are dimension is a no-regrets shortcut to winning together, defined by maximum trust and courage and a declaration that "the future belongs to us."

2. How We Work (Agility)

Once leaders have sharpened the Who We Are dimension, they must optimize for How We Work, the second dimension of the Trust Mindset. I watched *Working* on Netflix, presented by Barack Obama, the former president of the United States.[22] In the opening credits, he recalls discovering a book by chance called *Working: People Talk About What They Do All Day and How They Feel About What They Do* by Studs Terkel, a chronicle of people from every walk of life and what it was like for them to work. Paraphrasing Terkel, Obama says: "There is no one way to begin; it is arbitrary, but you want to find that quintessential truth. The essence of truth."[23]

The How We Work dimension answers, "Are we empowered to work as adults, or is 'fake empowerment' the default?" Fake empowerment means control over context and power over trust. It demands deference and erodes initiative. Organizations recognize and reward hippos (the highest-paid person's opinion) and hierarchies rather than impact and contribution. Fake empowerment is still the norm for many organizations. Hack Future Lab's research reveals that the five most prominent barriers to working with empowerment are:

1. Silos and lack of cross-functional collaboration

2. Slow decision-making

3. Lack of strategic clarity

4. Rigid processes

5. Formal hierarchies

Unilever is a 138,000-person firm known for iconic brands such as Ben & Jerry's, Hellman's, and Dove. The leadership team has committed to strengthening the How We Work dimension by launching a new Compass Organization called the Power of Five and The Focus of One. The goal is to simplify the business faster and become more agile with greater end-to-end accountability for P&L and operations. A Power of Five strategy simplifies the business model into five business groups, from Personal Care to Beauty and Well-being, leveraging scale and efficiency as one unified team.[24]

When I shared the stage at a conference with the former CEO of Unilever, he asked a question that every leader should ask, "How do we remove barriers to performance and make work more agile?" Hack Future Lab's research on the How We Work dimension shows that 63% of leaders report that a lack of agility is a barrier to organizational performance, and 57% of employees agree that "fake empowerment" is part of the culture.[25] Breaking down hierarchies and widespread agility are top concerns for leaders because most organizations still operate in the Industrial Age, not the Intelligence Age.

Here's how to get started:

- Move talent closer to where value creation is by getting the best people into the right roles at the right time and winning the race to reskill

- Evolve from managers of tasks to leaders of learning, breaking down hierarchies and committees so individuals can own their decisions and learn from them

- Move from micro-management and constant "checking" to continuous coaching, empowering, and improvement

- Clarify and strengthen decision rights and guardrails and give leaders full accountability for P&L and operations

- Reward and celebrate agile work more than bureaucratic work, streamline duplicative governance, remove management layers, and replace tick-boxing exercises with work that matters

Since Unilever's launch of the Compass Organization, it's been operationally nimbler and healthier, with lower overheads, increased productivity, and fewer mistakes. The How We Work dimension can be accelerated by creating a collective, bottom-up initiative to crowdsource the best questions and ideas for working with agility and intelligence. Google uses a Simplicity Sprint to prioritize the How We Work dimension, removing barriers to speed and execution.[26] Participating in the Sprint empowers people to own their part of the growth agenda and feel set up for success by discussing several questions.

- What would help us work with greater clarity to serve our customers?
- Where should we remove roadblocks and barriers to success to get better results faster?
- How do we eliminate waste, stay entrepreneurial, and focus on fast execution and growth?

Using the Simplicity Sprint to gather feedback on productivity and focus, Google gives every employee a voice that solving the How We Work challenge is a shared, collective team effort. "Dogfooding" is a tool where small, diverse Googlers pilot and test the product internally before widely rolling out new initiatives. This enables real-world feedback and flags issues before they become difficulties. Small experiments help minimize failure and maximize the chances of success. It's about everyone being trusted to find a faster, flatter, and more intelligent way of unlocking value and doing their best work, not just their busiest.[27]

Another side of the How We Work dimension is how decisions are made. Every leader I've met says they suffer from "decision fatigue." Hack Future Lab's search confirms that today's decisions are more complex than before, yet only a third of teams can link decision-making to enterprise value and strategy.[28] Inefficient decision-making wastes time and money and erodes trust, so what can leaders do to sustain high-speed, high-quality decision-making with a bias for action? Buurtzorg is a Dutch healthcare organization best described by what it lacks: fake empowerment, endless meetings, and broken rules and protocols that slow down decision-making and erode trust. Since it was founded in 2006, Buurtzorg has scaled a nurse-led holistic care model to more than 15,000 nurses and has revolutionized community care in the Netherlands with its higher purpose mission to prioritize "humanity over bureaucracy."[29] This means building ecosystems of trust and self-management and giving employees a strong sense of accountability and transparency for making things happen at the speed of the patient. Buurtzorg's successes come from a person or team with the freedom to step into the unknown and try something new, even if that means failure.

A vital aspect of the How We Work dimension at Buurtzorg is how decisions are made.

- **Focus on the game-changing ideas that matter.** Teams at Buurtzorg prioritize ideas and debate the ones with the most upside and the most downside. Sometimes, focusing on what makes an idea bad shines a spotlight on what might make the idea great. It's willful contrarianism.

- **At Buurtzorg, decisions are made, and lessons are learned.** They push decisions right to the "edge" and learn from their setbacks and mistakes. When they give power to the front line, individuals can make decisions and own the outcomes; trust and ownership increase and lazy excuses drop.

- **Give control to others and avoid short-term thinking.** Buurtzorg builds the How We Work muscle by breaking down silos and internal barriers, eliminating excess management layers, and removing useless metrics; this is vital for making work sustainable, enabling people to learn and grow.

- **Rethink how work gets done.** Finally, Buurtzorg has shown that despite its scale, it is possible to avoid slow decision-making and overreliance on meetings by rethinking how work gets done, who does the work, when it gets done, where it gets done, and what work is valued.[30]

The urgency for leaders to sharpen the How We Work dimension has been building for years before the rise of AI or the global pandemic. The lesson for leaders is that you can't be an agile organization without agile decision-making and a relentless focus on answering the How We Work question. How We Work is the ultimate purpose clarifier: Too many people are drowning in obsolete ways of working that are stuck in Industrial Age mindsets. They're not close to the customer and can't explore early signals for change because of internal barriers and a lack of freedom. It should be context over control, not control over context.

By giving new energy to the How We Work dimension of the Trust Mindset, leaders can unlock DELTAs (Distinct Elements of Trust and Autonomy) that make cultures more resilient and productive. The How We Work dimension of the Trust Mindset is essential for making human-led intelligence work an imperative in our organizations and saying goodbye to soul-sucking ways of working and stupid rules that make us feel like machines.

3. How We Grow (Scalability)

How We Grow is the final dimension of the Trust Mindset and is crucial for driving the business outside its comfort zone. Despite a complex legacy and challenging operational headwinds, it gives people a meaningful and actionable growth story they can believe in. Plans inform, but stories inspire. When leaders honor past achievements, define the present challenges, and inclusively shape the future growth story, people don't just feel included in the journey; they own their part of the future in a crystal clear and irresistible way.

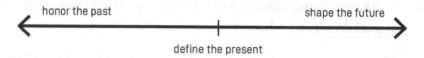

honor the past   shape the future

define the present

For most of my career, the future growth story was mostly fragmented, unclear, and lost in translation through short-termism, turf politics, jargon, and death by committee. Without a coherent and focused growth story and complete clarity of ownership, teams lack the macro perspective to guide their decisions and visibility about who should make those decisions and why.

How We Grow is inseparable from trust in each other because leaders can't hope to grow or transform without trust. Hack Future Lab's research shows that there is a big aspiration to action gap when it comes to how leaders activate the How We Grow dimension.

- 73% of employees are worried about the future and how it impacts them
- 66% of employees need clarification about their organizations' future growth story

- 58% of employees agree they are not co-leaders in their organization

- 54% of employees don't feel set up with the right mindsets or skill sets to own their part of the growth story

- 47% of employees agree that their work is more bureaucratic-led than growth-led

Source: Hack Future Lab

The How We Grow dimension challenges leaders to tell the future growth story expansively and inclusively, making it irresistible and crystal clear that we are "all in." The CEO of Adidas, Bjørn Gulden, is leading a remarkable turnaround driven by a relentless commitment to the How We Grow dimension.[31] Through defining the present and championing the future, he has ignited untapped growth muscles in everyone to lead themselves from the front (clarity of mind) and fight for daily growth (courage skills). A multiplier effect occurs when a person is asked to be a co-partner in the future growth story of the organization and will instinctively know how their role makes a difference: a bias for action soars, and teams mobilize around their best work and highest growth initiatives.

Hermès is a 186-year-old French luxury goods leader on a long-term mission to tackle the How We Grow dimension in the fashion industry. It wants to solve the vast waste issue in fashion and accusations that fashion companies are "profit-obsessed and nature uncaring" by fortifying the How We Grow dimension for the long term.[32] Tackling waste in the fashion industry is not just improving supply chains or offsetting carbon emissions. It demands rethinking and re-positioning the DNA of what an enterprise does, why it does it, and how it does it to be sustainable for the next generation.

Hermès has turned its How We Grow dimension into a platform for finding the upside in disruption. It has taken a courageous leap into the future by moving away from the original concept of luxury leather to Rishi, a leather alternative made from mycelium, the threadlike root structure of fungi, grown in trays by the California biotech start-up MycoWorks. Mycelium produces a strong cellular material that can be processed to produce an authentic leather effect.[33]

This smart bet on fungi-based leather is at the heart of Hermès's How We Grow dimension and means that by 2035, at least half of global revenues could be from nature-friendly, non-leather alternatives.[34] Hermès offers a powerful lesson in how an organization can renew itself repeatedly despite the burden of complexity and heavy legacy. The takeaway is that making a business sustainable and profitable is not mutually exclusive. Honoring the past, defining the present, and shaping the future are at the heart of the How We Grow dimension, separating growth leaders from the pack.

Here are some questions to consider to unlock the How We Grow dimension.

1. Do I clearly and consistently articulate our future growth story?

2. Do people feel trusted and empowered to own their part of the future growth story?

3. Does the future growth story enable leaders to link value across the enterprise and connect people to the most significant growth initiatives?

4. How do I remove internal barriers (e.g., bureaucracy, proxies, committees) to make the future growth story transparent, actionable, and inclusive?

5. What future growth headlines do we want to be written about, and is it clear and irresistible?

6. Finally, do we communicate and reinforce the future growth story in a way that honors our past successes, defines present challenges, and shapes our future priorities?

The final imperative of the Trust Mindset is to commit focus and energy to the How We Grow dimension. This is vital for building a profitable, sustainable, and trust-led future. Hack Future Lab's research shows that when all three dimensions of the Trust Mindset are awakened, companies demonstrate stronger bottom lines, happier workforces, and more loyal customers. Leaders who narrowly focus on financial impact and pay lip service to purpose, people, and the planet are the new outliers.

The Future of Trust

I had the chance to watch a game of ice hockey at the Scotiabank Arena, formerly known as Air Canada Centre, in a multipurpose arena located on Bay Street in the South Core district of Downtown Toronto. The game was remarkable to watch through the lens of how to win together through the power of collective trust. The game reminded me of the Canadian ice hockey legend Wayne Gretzky, who was asked why he was such an inventive player. Gretzky replied, "While other players skated to the puck, I skated to where the puck would be." That's how leaders must see the role of winning teams. They have an eye on the future, do the basics brilliantly, and win with trust. As I returned to my hotel, I wondered how many leaders and their teams skated to the puck rather than going to where the puck was going because trust is essential to lead through disruption.

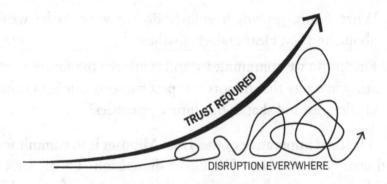

There is fear and hope as leaders pivot to remote and hybrid work models and humans and machines. Now is the time for leaders to reframe their trust narratives for a restless and complex future. Leaders must sharpen the Human Trust Agenda daily as beacons of trust, prioritizing trust across capabilities (how we do things) and cause (why we do things). Trust is and will continue to be the number one currency for tackling multiplying and overlapping issues, including:

- Building a human-led, tech-enabled workforce
- Winning the skills revolution
- Amplifying inclusivity and equity
- Hybrid work
- AI as a co-thinker in the organization
- Making well-being a central pillar of future readiness

Leaders who want to prepare for the future and strengthen existing potential should reflect on whether their leadership style is built for trust or fear-focused leadership. Trust-focused leadership is defined as a way of leading that inspires people to speak up (play to win) over silence (play to lose) and curiosity (great minds don't think alike) over conformity (great minds think alike). It demands respect and unlocks human brilliance.

Trust-focused companies like PayPal or BMW know the secret to a productive, flexible, and happy workforce: trust.

Fear-focused leadership is a way of leading that deters workers from challenging the status quo. It's a situation where people don't have the freedom or autonomy to make decisions that matter. It demands deference and downgrades human potential.

Here are three collective trust accelerators for leaders to turn workforce disruption into practical milestones for building agile, resilient, and trust-led futures.

1. Lead with trust

Leading with trust is a better alternative to control or coercion and the dreaded feedback sandwich that Professor Adam Grant describes: "Criticism between two slices of praise doesn't taste as good as it looks."[35] When we lead with trust, we signal that we care about the direction of the organization and its people and value a leadership style of care and co-creation, not command and control. Asking human-centric questions clarifies whether we are exceeding, meeting, or falling behind on leading with trust.

- Is trust our #1 value? If not, why now?

- Do we practice trust-focused or fear-focused leadership?

- Do you minimize or maximize trust and responsibility?

- Do we commodify or humanize trust?

- Do we obsess over trust, not just metrics?

- Do we make the invisible visceral?

- Do we hire on culture add or culture fit?

- Do we enable wise trust-based choices, not just the fastest?

- Do we bind trust to care and co-creation?

- Do we nurture and recognize trust in each other?

Pfizer is known for its race to make the impossible possible by creating the first COVID-19 vaccine in the world. You may not know that it's on a mission to make trust count by bringing its values to life in a personalized way (courage, equity, excellence, and joy at work).[36] The result is trust at the speed of science in the form of:

- Ecosystems of trust and ecosystems of talent: Reskilling, cross-skilling, and upskilling all employees with future-fit skills by 2025

- No-fail trust based on high-risk tolerance for learning, experimentation, and productive failures

- Trust-based leadership using new metrics for return on intelligence in addition to financial ones

- Winning together by role-modeling and sharing stories of learning and unlearning through reflection, feed forward, recognition, and celebration

Pfizer understands that making trust a top leadership priority is challenging in a world where humans are distracted and overloaded. Still, it's a simple decision if we want people to radiate purpose and care and feel they belong.

2. Adopt a listening mindset

When was the last time you felt truly listened to? Like me, you might be struggling to think of a recent example. Feeling listened to is the ultimate generosity in an age of fragmented attention spans, endless scrolling, and constant interruptions that force us to multitask. Leaders must "listen to learn" rather than "listen to win": We are fully present when we listen to learn. We declare, "I trust and respect you and want to understand you." Listening to win is the opposite. It's ego-focused rather than solution-focused. Listening to learn is a problem-solving tool because we hear what's not being said. "Do you have the opportunity to do your best work every day?" There's probably no question more critical for leaders to ask in organizations today.

People have long understood that most acts of creation are collaborative. Listening to each other sparks generosity and reciprocity, crucial for problem-solving, leadership, and teamwork. Look at what happened when two musicians, John Lennon and Paul McCartney, co-wrote music together. When humans are focused and intentional in their listening and collaboration efforts, there is a trust dividend: Teams report feeling more energized, supportive, and committed to the growth story and the mission.

For leaders, the stakes are high but worth it if we appeal to a higher purpose. Namely, our teams will feel a sense of mission, but they will also hold us accountable for our big decisions. They become proactive "outside-in" teams closer to the customer rather than reactive "inside-out" teams held captive to tick-box exercises and excess bureaucracy. Accountability and a bias for action increase because a thick layer of respect is at the core of listening. As organizations evolve from hierarchies to networks of teams, trust has also shifted from vertical trust (command and control) to horizontal trust (care and co-creation). Less control requires better listening skills and context or "ripple intelligence" if ideas are to travel faster across the business. Listening creates trust bonds between humans that strengthen context and a shared reality of the future. So, are you a good listener?

The problem is humans are highly distractable, and this makes listening problematic. I met a doctor who said the number of selfie-related accidents in A&E had increased more than 7X in one year. This matters because trust and clarity drop when leaders are not fully present and shun a listening mindset. Hack Future Lab's research shows that "66% of employees agree that listening is not a core strength in our organizations," while 84% of leaders believe that "listening is a strength."[37] How can leaders adopt a continuous listening mindset for connectivity, belonging, and trust to soar?

At JPMorgan Chase, a continuous listening strategy makes people feel good and think that their work matters and that they are co-partners in the growth story.[38]

- How often do you get the opportunity to do your best work?
- What would help us work with greater clarity and energy?
- What do you need from me to do your boldest work?
- What's not being said that should be said?
- How would you like to grow in this organization?

A listening mindset is a clear leadership edge: with wave after wave of disruptions on the rise, listening, feeling, connecting, and asking the right questions can engender a team's trust in the future, manage the present, and create a collective sense of "we're in this together." That's the essence of future readiness and a source code for purpose, mutual trust, and respect.

3. BYOD (bring your own divergence)

Why are only 5% of nations led by women, less than 8% of CEOs on the S&P 500 Index are women, and 23 are named John?[39] It's impossible to harness trust if diversity is not a strength. And when I say diversity and inclusion, I don't just mean gender diversity (more women in the boardroom). Don't be fooled by conformity. Although leaders may feel more comfortable with people who look and sound the same, it can lead to echo chambers, the curse of sameness, and tunnel vision thinking, which are the enemies of creativity and innovation.

From cultural to cognitive diversity, how leaders embrace differences is a shortcut to team collaboration, better decision-making, and improved financial performance. Hack Future Lab's research shows that companies with above-average diversity scores reported higher returns on innovation and Return on Intelligence, a new human metric for collective impact [40]

Many organizations have complex, legacy cultures with a homogenous leadership team. BYOD is the antidote and means leading with maximum divergence and maximum trust.

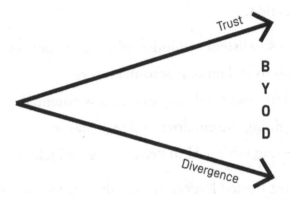

Building a diverse workforce is essential to any organization's disruption and future readiness. Hack Future Lab's research shows that BYOD teams see a 70% improvement in decision-making and problem-solving, ultimately leading to healthier, happier cultures and increased profits. Leaders who sustain BYOD principles capture the most value and trust from differences, divergent thinking, and diversity.[41]

- **Differences:** Do we focus on leveraging differences, not difficulties, and recognize and celebrate an inclusive and agility-led culture?

- **Divergent thinking:** Do we share divergent points of view and willingness to lean in more boldly to challenge old ways of thinking?

- **Diversity:** Do we take the initiative and proactively increase diversity across all dimensions of the enterprise, starting with the C-suite?

Accenture, the business consultancy, has been ranked number one on Refinitiv's Diversity and Inclusion Index, which tracks publicly traded companies with the most diverse and inclusive workplaces.[42] Leaders embrace the principle that people want values in their organizations and practice human-centered leadership grounded in the 4Cs: Care, Commitment, Contribution, and Co-creation.

- An inclusive listening mindset where everyone is a co-thinker
- Less micro and more macro-managers
- From imposter syndrome to limitless potential
- Reimagining the employee value proposition
- Harnessing ethical AI to drive hiring and talent mobility

The most trusted leaders capture the most value when difference, divergent thinking, and diversity are not just a set of beliefs but are recognized, measured, and celebrated. People want values and values at work, starting with belief and belonging to each other. When more employees are constantly in job-search mode, and talent scarcity is worsening, all future-fit organizations must prioritize BYOD because it's the right thing to do and a wise business decision.

Trust Is The Ultimate Human Currency

People want to work in organizations that make them feel fulfilled and alive: human-led, intentionally diverse, purpose and trust-driven, and built for speed. The bad news is that every engagement study year after year shows that many firms are failing them badly. Hack Future Lab's estimates show that only 57% of leaders worldwide are "actively trusted," and 33% of employees strongly agree "I trust a stranger more than my boss."[43] Too many humans are unhappy at work. Perhaps AI will be the never-seen-before opportunity to reawaken the leader in all of us.

If leaders consider "the one thing they could do differently today to help their people be prepared for the future," where would you start? I would suggest trust. With economic headwinds and AI disruption an everyday reality, the best strategy is to bake trust into the DNA of leadership, culture, performance, and talent. People want to thrive in trust-based cultures that don't practice "kiss up and kick down" behaviors and endure "feedback sandwiches" and performance reviews that are tick-boxing exercises. It's dehumanizing. A mandate for nurturing and growing sustained trust has never been more critical to unlocking the untapped potential of humans. Are we ready to become a leader of trust and shape the future with wise and bold intentionality?

Takeaways

- **Make trust your North Star:** Nietzsche said, "The most common form of human blindness is forgetting why we do what we do." Leadership fails because of a lack of collective purpose and trust. It is vital to the future of leadership to understand how to earn, cultivate, and leverage purpose and trust. We all know that trust in leaders is not a success story. In the age of AI misinformation, inequality, and ethics breaches, trust is the best human currency for helping others embrace evolution and win the future together: connection, community, care, and commitment. Harness the Trust Mindset dimensions of Who We Are (Identity),

How We Work (Agility), and How We Grow (Scalability) to elevate trust and purpose in each other and be better prepared to make trust our guide for awakening the superpowers of **Believing, Belonging, Braving, and Becoming** in our people.

- **Get out of echo chambers:** Cultures of conformity are hardwired to keep us in our bubbles, never challenged by disagreement, and never required to think that we might be wrong. We would do well to remember that most of our opinions are not as informed and well rounded as we believe and be humble enough to accept that we may be wrong sometimes. Listening, questioning, bridge-building, and speaking up rather than choosing silence is the essence of deep authenticity and the best guardrails against cultures of conformity that reject ideas that challenge the status quo. Leaders reduce the risk of being trapped in zombie echo chambers by sharing divergent points of view and testing and challenging the always-done ways. Self-awareness could be the meta-skill of the post-AI era: Adopting a continuous listening mindset builds empathy and belonging and signals to others that "I care about your learning and growth in this organization." It's about doing well by doing good.

- **No-fail trust:** The best way to demystify the workforce or AI-driven disruption is to embrace a culture of "no-fail trust." It takes a culture of care and tolerance for mistakes to find the upside in disruption, but a wait-and-see strategy is not a good idea if you are learning at the speed of the customer. Now, it's test and learn. A client I worked with (let's call them Delta Coffee) decided to introduce AI and machine learning into their coffee store to analyze how productive the staff was, from receiving a coffee order to preparing and serving the coffee. Within a month of introducing AI, the speed of serving coffee had increased by 33%, but the CEO had not expected that the quality would decline. Worse, the motivation of the employees fell off a cliff because they felt they were working in a surveillance culture: Empathy for customers dropped in the pursuit of speed and efficiency, and the overall experience for customers was worse. Without a culture of no-fail trust, it's impossible to take risks or test hypotheses about turning disruption into an upside, such as how to work alongside AI in a way that protects our dignity and enhances well-being and productivity.

- **Well-being as a central pillar:** It's impossible to earn and sustain daily trust if we're burned out or suffering from meta-anxiety. Leaders are tired and distracted. Brain fog. Meetings fatigue. Volatility fatigue. Innovations like social media and AI promise to democratize information, empower choice, and increase human connection, but we should pay attention to the risk of "artificial idiocy" and "artificial intimacy." For example, three-quarters of the world's population is connected to the internet.[44] Yet, we face a loneliness crisis and runaway inequality, and social media has weaponized fake news, eroding the well-being and trust in our firms, institutions, and democracies. What's our return on well-being? Extractive attention business models and bot-manipulated social media exploit our basic instinct to belong and can undermine our ultimate leadership resources: trust and attention.

6

Beyond Is Where We Begin

"The limits of the possible can only be defined by going
beyond them into the impossible."

– **Arthur C. Clarke**

J esse Armstrong is one of my heroes. He is the creator of the
HBO series *Succession*. This American satirical black comedy-
drama series follows the power struggles of the fictional Roy
Family, who control Waystar RoyCo, an elite global media and
entertainment conglomerate. As the series unfolds, we witness
the escalating conflicts within the Roy family, broken alliances,
and the characters' true motivations uncovered. Some memorable quotes include, "You can't make a Tomelette without breaking some Gregs," and "You make your reality. And once you've
done it, everyone believes it was all so f-ing obvious." While the
brutal and funny unpicking of a wealthy dysfunctional family,
manic deal-making, and desire for control is entertaining to
watch, Armstrong's journey on the roots of *Succession* offers valuable lessons to leaders searching for the upside in disruption.
I heard Armstrong speak in person at a Financial Times Ideas
Festival, where he recounted his first vivid memory of *Succession*,
that he was certain it was a dud and would fail, and that the obstacles to getting a "yes" to the pitch by producers were enormous.
He recounted how driving ourselves outside our comfort zones
despite the urge to give up is deeply ingrained in the journey of
embracing the unknown and that it starts with what we hold true.

Over the last few years, three truths that are undeniably clear
to leaders searching for the upside in disruption have emerged.

First, When Disruption Is the Norm, Rethinking Is the Answer

Leaders must embrace the upside in disruption to avoid zombie
leadership and the curse of sameness because no organization is
immune from the forces of disruption. A rethinking mindset is a

form of proactive resilience: it anticipates volatility as a tailwind for learning, growth, and opportunity. We must rethink everything in the leadership value chain: culture, talent, strategy, and execution. Without it, it's impossible to create an agile culture because rethinking brings new and unexpected ideas necessary during uncertain times and encourages us to prepare our future readiness about what's emerging or eroding in our leadership. As the rate of disruption accelerates, so must the rate of rethinking, pushing the organization to step outside its comfort zone and fully embrace continuous evolution.

I interviewed with the Nordic Business Forum, discussing why rethinking matters more than sameness. It's the key to unlocking the door to new worlds and helping us see the future differently to seize the upside; untested assumptions can be heavy and slow us down. It starts with imagining what the future success story looks like for you. One of the defining strengths of tennis player Novak Djokovic is his ability to bounce back from extreme adversity and vividly imagine a future success story. He shows the hunger to push through impossible limits (e.g., aging) and turn stress into a platform for boldness. In a world of accelerating change, the best leaders don't just react to the future. They harness it as a platform to get hungrier, wiser, and better.

Hack Future Lab's research shows a "resilience dividend" for those who sharpen their future readiness muscle. They're 1.8x more likely to outperform their peers and 3.4x less likely to burn out in a crisis.[1] When we're deeply trusted to scale our boldest selves, it's easier to say "no," cut through the noise, and focus on our top priorities.

A great starting point is to ask, "What 'success headlines' do I want to achieve?" Start by glimpsing into the future and asking yourself what you want to achieve by this time next year. What do you want them to say about your leadership impact when you read the headlines? What will be your boldest moments? What mindset shifts and choices will you make to turn disruption into an upside? What should you rethink and unlearn to stay relevant for tomorrow's world? What are the mindset shifts, assumptions, and risks for this journey? Let these future milestones determine your goals and the changes you must make. Think ahead, just a few years, to 2027: What accomplishments do you want to reflect on three years from now? What future do you want to create and why?

Re-thinking – becoming aware of something new in existing contexts and noticing the organization's blind spots – is crucial for sustainable performance despite disruption. In today's rapidly changing world, knowledge and competitive advantage quickly become irrelevant, and leaders can be sidetracked by past successes. Starbucks has evolved from being a coffeehouse chain to a lifestyle brand, expanding its menu offerings, introducing mobile ordering and payment systems, and emphasizing sustainability initiatives like ethically sourced coffee and recyclable packaging.[2] Without embracing rethinking, our expertise and assumptions become obsolete, making us prisoners of our past success. This hampers our ability to be future-ready. The greatest challenge is that most humans think linearly, which is the wrong game in a world of hyperscale and counterintuitive strategies. Rethinking reminds everybody the future is not linear but exponential and that you can't have resilient leadership without deliberate and sustained rethinking.

Second, Technology Changes Fast. Humans Don't

Co-intelligence means learning to work alongside AI, yet one of our time's most significant leadership paradoxes is that technology changes fast, but humans don't.

Leaders are trapped in a wisdom gap with the complexities of runaway AI, outstripping our Paleolithic human brains' capacity to make sense of it all (e.g., consider the processing power of a computer chip has increased more than a trillion times since the 1950s).[3] Still, the brain's processing power hasn't. Data is just bits of information. Knowledge is connecting the bits of information. Wisdom is turning data into new and unexpected insights, and this is where we should invest more of our attention. If you think bullshit is an issue in organizations, wait until you experience "botshit" as AI brings the costs of bullshit to zero.[4] While technology isn't the only reason, runaway AI rapidly widens the wisdom gap fueled by always-on cultures and overloaded brains.

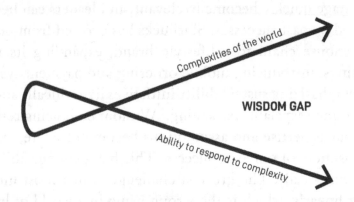

Too many humans are sleepwalking at work. Will AI be the never-seen-before opportunity to reawaken the leader in all of us? Leaders are overloaded and distracted by smartphones and millions of apps that kill time rather than save time. Innovations like social media and AI promise to democratize information, empower choice, and increase human connection, but we should pay attention to the rise of shallow work and transactional relationships.

Maybe we need to take a strategic pause; a leader's attention is a limited resource, and we are highly distractable creatures; it's easier than ever to be busy but unproductive, and how we use technology is to blame. How many emails and messages are you receiving every day? According to EarthWeb, in the United States, more than 350 billion emails are sent and received daily, and the average leader deals with 30,000 emails and text messages a year.[5] For some, it's 300 messages daily (Slack, WhatsApp, email). Economist Herbert A. Simon was right when he described attention as a "bottleneck" in human thinking: "In an information-rich world, the wealth of information means a dearth of something else: a scarcity of whatever it is that information consumes. What information consumes is rather obvious: it consumes the attention of its recipients. Hence, a wealth of information creates a poverty of attention."[6]

Notifications constantly hijack our attention, fooling us into thinking something trivial is urgent and downgrading our human potential and leadership focus.

To avoid being overwhelmed by runaway technology, we must invest time in humans, not just technology. It's about protecting our attention and remaining deeply human in a data-hungry world. To avoid AI adoption causing excess fear and anxiety (a performance killer), take an intentional and human-centric approach: adopt a co-creation strategy for AI and share stories, early wins, and metrics to objectively evaluate the hidden risks and unintended consequences of using AI. Leaders must show zero compromises on making AI ethical, fair, transparent, and safe and protect our most valuable asset: trust.

Third, In the Human-Technology Nexus, Courage Skills Are the New Leadership

Behavioral scientist and author Rory Sutherland said, "The next revolution is not technological; it's psychological."[7] Overthinking is a big problem in most organizations, creating risk aversion and bottlenecks that become silos or barriers to agility. Future anxiety is one of the most significant types of overthinking, with the acceleration of AI as a potential disruptor of jobs and security.

Waiting for complete certainty is risky in an era of acceleration and change. We can't lean into the future, navigate tech disruption, or turn volatility into value creation without sharpening our courage skills: Proactive, pro-change, pro-growth, pro-resilience. Hack Future Lab's research shows that 66% of employees agree that their organizations are conformists. We can't thrive in the Intelligence Age if our organizations are comprised of sameness and conformists.[8] Nike's reinvention has been characterized by making bold moves in digital innovation, sustainability, product excellence, and powerful branding strategies and staying true to its core values of daring, excellence, and courage.[9] Great ideas happen when people put their courage to work, whether it's complexity reduction across the business, launching a new business model, or investing aggressively in sustainable new growth pathways. How would your organization rate its return on courage (ROC)? Is it exceeding or behind expectations? The Intelligence Age means adopting a beginner's mindset and a spirit of boldness. The most significant risk to the long-term vitality of most companies is not new competitors, market volatility, or tech disruption. It's a lack of courage.

I partnered with a technology client (let's call it Zeta) that wanted to sharpen its courage skills for an emerging world of new competitors, new customers, and new technologies by introducing Future-Fit month. More than 14,000 employees worldwide can access virtual and in-person "future readiness" skills like how to work alongside AI and turn data into insights. The outcome is that attendees can curate their courage journey to become courageous thinkers and doers. Now, they are inspired to find their personal upside in disruption from working in radically different ways to exploring new skills and career pathways.

Beware of the Rubber Band Effect

The rubber band effect is a common phenomenon I've become aware of over the last few years. It works when a leadership team attends a conference or meeting to be inspired by new thinking, fresh perspectives, and ambitious priorities. The collective goodwill and intention are well meaning. Everybody goes "all in" during those few days together, and the attendees make the customary declarations about follow-up plans, actions, and deadlines. Everybody says the "right things" during the group's time together, and bold commitments are made after the session. The problem is the rubber band effect. Mindsets are stretched during the meeting, concerns are voiced, and aspirations abound, yet when individuals arrive home after a long-haul flight, their rubber band has snapped back into the same place as before the meeting.

Nothing has changed, or not enough, to avoid relapsing into the always-done ways that no longer serve the future or create value. Leadership inertia and "somebody's else's problem" syndrome follow: ideas get lost. Plans become spreadsheets, and the bureaucratic BS goes up again. To overcome the rubber band effect, leaders must break the bias for déjà vu conversations and the curse of zombie ideas that afflicts every organization and adopt against-the-grain approaches to change, disrupting from within. There is safety in the herd, and alignment is essential, but we also need to be on the watch for groupthink.

The last thing a CEO needs is to be surrounded by "yes" people, however tempting that is. The herd mentality forces leaders to defend obsolete strategies or points of view about the future that no longer hold. Take the story of Yahoo, which arguably missed the opportunity to pivot to the future and seize the Intelligence Age. Yahoo passed over the chance to acquire Google for $1 billion and buy Facebook for an alleged $1.1 billion.[10] Brad Garlinghouse, the former Yahoo SVP, wrote in an internal memo: "I've heard our strategy described as spreading peanut butter across the myriad opportunities that continue to evolve in the online world. The result is a thin layer of investment spread across everything we do; thus, we focus on nothing. I wouldn't say I like peanut butter. We all should." The leadership lacked execution certainty and got sidetracked by short-term band-aids, silo behaviors, and paralysis by analysis. Every organization is one step away from this must-avoid scenario. Without a coherent "no" strategy, Yahoo leadership wanted to do everything and please everyone but never took steps to declare clearly what they were and were not.[11]

When they did communicate, it was mostly to fight over ownership, status, and internal proxies. I see this happening in organizations everywhere. Despite its creation during the dot-com years and being valued at more than $125 billion at its peak, Yahoo needed to reinvent itself with the urgency that disruption demands, and Verizon bought it for just $4.8 billion.[12] Its demise reminds us that every organization is not immune to becoming obsolete when leaders fail to update the mindsets and choices for a radically different world.

Willful contrarianism explicitly takes a point of view about the future that runs counter to conventional business wisdom and is a powerful antidote to Industrial Age thinking. It's a bias buster. If no one explores a contrarian view, the firm may miss opportunities for innovation or long-term success. For example, one firm I worked with leveraged its "fear of becoming obsolete" to take the role of an activist investor. The leadership team tapped into its psychological capital to test its future readiness muscle and, in so doing, turned many of the mindsets and assumptions it was clinging to upside down. The team worked with external customers and operations heads from relevant business units to create arguments supporting or opposing the launch of a new business model. Participants were asked to consider the long-term consequences of the decision and the potential reactions from employees, competitors, and investors. Worse-case scenarios, advanced analytics, and crowd-sourcing were utilized to assess the likely responses of the herd to a decision. This led to bold moves around how they operate and their future growth story, reaffirming a collective commitment to winning the future together.

The Dogs That Don't Bark

Going against the crowd can be a daunting experience in any context. When it comes to reputation, it can be paralyzing. Leaders must acknowledge the presence of herd mentality and actively seek out opposing views to break free from it. The "dogs that don't bark" is a phrase that means, even with good intentions, leaders can fall victim to cognitive and organizational biases and stay silent when they should be speaking up. The Volkswagen emissions scandal was a watershed moment highlighting the importance of accountability and ethical issues in the automotive sector. It served as a wake-up call for the industry, regulators, and consumers, prompting greater scrutiny of emissions testing procedures and encouraging a reassertion of why ethical leadership matters. Most organizations are only a few steps away from their own "Dieselgate" and should bake transparency into the DNA of everything they do.[13]

The success fallacy is another bias whereby leaders are seduced by the assumption that the current strategy is repeatable until it isn't. And, of course, that tended to be true in a stable and predictable world. Once a retail powerhouse, Sears struggled to adapt to the rise of e-commerce and changing consumer shopping habits. The firm maintained an extensive network of physical stores while competitors like Amazon thrived online. Sears's failure to invest in e-commerce and update its stores resulted in declining sales and store closures, ultimately leading to bankruptcy.[14] The success fallacy means leaders become prisoners of the mindsets and frameworks of their current success and struggle to test their assumptions with a different lens.

While there is comfort in sticking with what we know, a firm may miss out on opportunities for long-term growth if no one on the team challenges the prevailing mindset of the day. Although it may be difficult to change mindsets completely, leaders who take a contrarian stance can use counter-factual thinking to pressure-test their ideas and biases before making critical business decisions.

Frontier Leadership

Recent economic and geopolitical disruptions have blown up traditional thinking, and we always underestimate the risk of standing still. Now, we must become frontier leaders: improvising, adapting, and overcoming obstacles with the curiosity to explore and the courage to rethink and unlearn. Leadership historically has been hierarchy-led (control, power, and rules) over frontier-led (trust, care, and co-creation). The challenge is that leaders are experiencing an extended period of what anthropologists call liminality or paradigm-shifting, an in-between world suspended between the certainties of the past and the possibilities of the future. Frontier leadership starts with reimagining what an AI-driven future means for us and our workforce and is crucial for long-term growth and resilience. SpaceX, officially known as Space Exploration Technologies Corp., has revolutionized the aerospace industry through its groundbreaking

technology and relentless pursuit of space exploration. It operates with a culture of rapid iteration and innovation, constantly
pushing the boundaries of what is possible in spaceflight.

Since SpaceX began flying the Falcon 9 rocket, the cost of
launch per pound has decreased from $10,000 per kilogram
to roughly $2,500.00. The leadership team embraces failure as a
natural part of the learning process and iterates quickly to
improve its technology and capabilities. This approach has enabled SpaceX to achieve remarkable feats relatively quickly and
maintain its position as a leader in the aerospace industry.[15]

Being bold means, by definition, accepting the risk of failure,
and it's natural to fear the unknown. Sometimes, it brings worry
and doubt; other times, it sparks curiosity, possibility, and discovery.
Our mindset and attitude toward risk and the unknown are crucial
in leadership and helping others find the upside in disruption.
Without it, leaders struggle to pivot from a "wait and see" to "challenge and grow." Too much certainty and we risk becoming stuck
in strategies of sameness, doing the same as our industry peers and
a race to the bottom; too much uncertainty can erode our well-
being and force us into panic mode rather than growth. Embracing
the fear of the unknown as validation that we are growing is a helpful way to turn doubt into daring and risk into upside.

This happened in my own life. I used to work in the safe and predictable world of consulting. I had my life mapped out to retirement. For many years, I was grateful for the progression of my career and found the work intellectually challenging and meaningful. I came from a family of hard workers who stayed in the same firm for many decades because that's what you did and what the world expected. Since then, everything has changed. We've moved from traditional career climbing walls to flexible projects and mentorships where it's feasible that our children will live one-hundred-year lives and have multiple cross-industry skills and work experiences.

Whatever the future holds, people will still want to thrive in human-led, trust-based cultures that combine meaning, choice, and opportunity over a lifetime. When I look back, I realize that in my former career in consulting, the moment arrived when I was no longer growing, and my work had become too rigid and predictable. I was on autopilot but had normalized that feeling to the point of feeling numb about what I needed to change but couldn't because of the fear of the unknown. Remaining in a place of stagnation felt safer than making a courageous leap into the future. While I was responsible for my life choices, the world I had grown up in had also inadvertently squeezed out my capacity to seize the future boldly and understand that beyond is where you begin. One day, it would take a life-changing accident to reawaken my relationship with the unknown and find the upside in disruption.

On a cold winter's day, I decided to visit a store in the market town of Stratford-upon-Avon, the birthplace of Shakespeare. Suddenly, there was a massive explosion, and I woke up to the sound of desperate screams and panic all around me. Was it a bomb attack? I couldn't move and could smell a burning tire on my leg, my flesh slowly melting underneath it. A car driver had lost control, mounted the sidewalk, and crashed into the store, running over any person who happened to be in its way. It's a miracle nobody died that day, and I was lucky enough to survive a life-changing accident. In an interview, Mike Tyson, a marvel of reinvention, from podcast host to actor, once said, "Everyone has a plan until they get punched in the mouth." It took the ultimate disruption – a life-threatening accident and full-circle moment – to wake me up about who I was and who I wanted to become as a leader and as a human being. This should not be the playbook to push us through inertia to start thinking and feeling intentionally about what our purpose and hoped-for legacy in life are!

Research shows that toward the end of our lives, the regret of inaction outnumbers the regret of action, and one of the top regrets among leaders is a lack of boldness.[16] Today's leadership challenges can't be solved with traditional thinking or conventional strategies. It will require boldness of heart and courage of ideas. Humans' brains are hardwired to spot the risk and are lousy at missing the upside. Not long ago, I was honored to meet a 100-year-old lady whose mantra is "no regrets." She was born in 1924, after the First World War and the Spanish Flu, which killed more than 50 million humans. Her dream was to study mathematics at university, but the odds were stacked against her. The societal pressures to conform, coupled with the onset of the Great Depression, meant many women were discouraged from attending college because society instilled in them the belief that pursuing careers would take away employment opportunities from men who needed to provide for their families. The Great Depression created a new lost generation as more people, especially women, gave up their hopes of attending university.[17]

When I met with her for a coffee, she shared her story of discovering the upside of disruption and how changes always come wrapped up as risk and opportunity. She waited until age 83 to announce a family meeting and declare that she would apply to university to study for a Bachelor of Arts in Mathematics. The first reaction of the family was shock. How could their 83-year-old grandmother contemplate attending university at such an age? When she applied, her biggest fear was not getting a place. About two months passed, and then, one morning, a letter arrived. The university accepted her application. Three years later, when she graduated, she was twice as old as the professor. This could have been the end of the story, but once we discover the upside of disruption, it's unstoppable. At age 89, she had another family meeting. The family was anxious and didn't know what to expect. She announced that it was time to do a master's and that there "was no time to lose." Fast forward to 100 years, and she called another family meeting. This time, she declared that one of her goals was to do a parachute jump, and a 100-year milestone was the right moment. She showed me photos of her jumping from a plane for a tandem dive at more than 8,000 ft. She did it twice. Before I said goodbye to her, I asked her about her plans for her next birthday when she reached 101. She smiled and looked at me, "If I'm lucky to be still alive, I want to swim with great white sharks in South Africa – but don't tell my family."

For the 100-year-old lady, despite the 1920s being known for a severe global economic downturn and incalculable human suffering, it was also a decade of major inventions and medical breakthroughs such as insulin, vitamins, and penicillin. New technologies and the ingenuity and resilience of humans led to the discovery of life-changing vaccines for diseases such as scarlet fever, polio, and tuberculosis – a disease more lethal than COVID-19. As the story of the 100-year-old lady showed, the regret of inaction is a powerful calling for finding the upside in disruption, and the opposite of knowing isn't always ignorance. It can be a wonder. Novelist Haruki Murakami wrote, "Once the storm is over, you won't remember how you made it through or managed to survive. You won't even be sure whether the storm is over. But one thing is certain. You won't be the same person who walked in when you come out of the storm." Whatever the future holds, as Sam Altman's sign says, "Nobody knows what is going to happen." Is that scary? Yes. Is that exciting? Yes. But it's also a call to reflection and a call to courage to embrace the unknown and unlock the limitless potential of the upside of disruption.

The DARE Leadership Test

"Only when we are brave enough to explore the darkness will we discover the infinite power of our light."

– Brené Brown

Economist John Kenneth Galbraith said, "There are two kinds of forecasters: those who don't know, and those who don't know they don't know." Leaders should avoid assuming that the future is just about technology and trends. It's about mindset shifts and behaviors, too. Leaders must search for the upside in disruption to avoid herd mentality and the curse of sameness because our leadership challenges can't be solved with yesterday's assumptions. The DARE (Data, Agility, Risk, and Evolution) Leadership Test is a simple tool to identify your existing strengths and gaps. To be more informed, you may want to get feedback from others on how they see you. For each dimension, score your future readiness levels on a scale from 1 (low) to 5 (high). A score of 3 or below for each statement indicates a priority area for action. Ask, "How will I build capability in this specific gap to ensure sustained future readiness?"

Data

Lead with AI

I am experimenting with AI as a co-pilot	1	2	3	4	5
I am curiosity-driven about emerging tech	1	2	3	4	5
I use AI to automate and elevate my work	1	2	3	4	5
I understand the risks of AI	1	2	3	4	5
I am future ready	1	2	3	4	5

Agility

Great Leaders Unlearn

I make unlearning a priority	1	2	3	4	5
I eliminate bureaucratic BS	1	2	3	4	5
I use failure as a tool for learning	1	2	3	4	5
I know my must-win priorities	1	2	3	4	5
I learn at the speed of the customer	1	2	3	4	5

Risk

The Courage Advantage

I champion the future growth story	1	2	3	4	5
I search for the upside in disruption	1	2	3	4	5
I have high execution certainty	1	2	3	4	5
I model courage over conformity	1	2	3	4	5
I have a strong future readiness muscle	1	2	3	4	5

Evolution

In Trust, We Grow

I make trust my #1 value	1	2	3	4	5
I radiate purpose	1	2	3	4	5
I empower others to scale	1	2	3	4	5
I make change happen	1	2	3	4	5
I create committed direction	1	2	3	4	5

Notes

Chapter 1

1. "This Experience May Feel Futuristic: Three Rides in Waymo Robot Taxi," *New York Times*, August 21, 2023, https://www.nytimes.com/2023/08/21/technology/waymo-driverless-cars-san-francisco.html.
2. "Davos 2024: Sam Altman on the future of AI," WEF, January 18, 2024. https://www.weforum.org/agenda/2024/01/davos-2024-sam-altman-on-the-future-of-ai/.
3. "Future Readiness Insights," Hack Future Lab, November 2023. The survey was conducted in the field with Hack Future Lab's proprietary survey panel from July 17, 2023, to August 8, 2023. It garnered responses from 611 participants in the United States representing a range of regions, industries, company sizes, and functional specialties.
4. "The Increasing Importance of a Best Friend at Work," Gallup, August 17,2022,https://www.gallup.com/workplace/397058/increasing-importance-best-friend-work.aspx.
5. "China's new 'tang ping' trend aims to highlight pressures of work culture," BBC, June 3, 2021, https://www.bbc.co.uk/news/world-asia-china-57348406.
6. "How Hemingway Gradually – Then Suddenly – Defined the Zeitgeist," *Wired*, July 8, 2022, https://www.wired.com/story/plaintext-hemingway-gradually-suddenly-zeitgeist/.
7. "Eternal You: A Horrifying Doc About AI Companies Recreating the Dead," *Rolling Stone*, January 20, 2024, https://www.rollingstone.com/tv-movies/tv-movie-reviews/eternal-you-doc-sundance-ai-digital-afterlife-death-chatgpt-technology-1234950589/.
8. "Fortune favors the bold," Wikipedia, https://en.wikipedia.org/wiki/Fortune_favours_the_bold.
9. "Future Readiness Insights," Hack Future Lab, November 2023.

10. "Planetary Thinking: Philosopher Yuk Hui asks how art can transform technology," *Nordic Art Review*, November 11, 2021, https://kunstkritikk.com/planetary-thinking/.

11. "BlackBerry film hails the must-have gadget that the iPhone turned into a forgotten relic," EL PAIS, May 11, 2023, https://english.elpais.com/culture/2023-05-10/blackberry-film-hails-the-must-have-gadget-that-the-iphone-turned-into-a-forgotten-relic.html#.

12. "Is your strategy good enough to move you up on the power curve?" McKinsey & Company, January 30, 2018, https://www.mckinsey.com/capabilities/strategy-and-corporate-finance/our-insights/the-strategy-and-corporate-finance-blog/is-your-strategy-good-enough-to-move-you-up-on-the-power-curve.

13. "Big Tech stocks' massive gains this year have made them even more dominant. That could be bad news for investors," *Business Insider*, May 29, 2023, https://markets.businessinsider.com/news/stocks/big-tech-stocks-apple-microsoft-alphabet-amazon-nvidia-meta-charts-2023-5.

14. "Europe's 'Granolas' Fuel Record Stock Market Surge," *Financial Times*, February 23, 2024, https://www.ft.com/content/b87e7bd6-b2be-43ca-bf03-a221383a8a92.

15. "Talent and Awe," Stuart Crainer and Des Dearlove, Thinkers50, March 4, 2024 https://thinkers50.com/blog/talent-award-2017-shortlist/.

16. "The man who predicted the Great Resignation has more big news," *Financial Times*, April 3, 2022, https://www.ft.com/content/3e561d41-0267-4d40-9c30-01e62fa9c10f.

17. "Future Readiness Insights," Hack Future Lab, November 2023.

18. "Reskilling Revolution: Preparing 1 billion people for tomorrow's economy," WEF, January 17, 2024, https://www.weforum.org/impact/reskilling-revolution-reaching-600-million-people-by-2030/.

19. "Moore's Law: The past, present, and future of Gordon Moore's golden rule for the semiconductor industry," Intel Corporation Inc., September 18, 2023, https://www.intel.com/content/www/us/en/newsroom/resources/moores-law.html.

20. "Inside Peloton's rapid rise and bitter fall – and its attempt at a comeback," CNBC, February 19, 2023, https://www.cnbc.com/2023/02/19/peloton-rise-fall-attempted-comeback.html.

21. "Liquid Death's Recyclable Packaging Provides an Alternative to Bottled Water," The Cool Down, January 4, 2024, https://www.thecooldown.com/green-business/liquid-death-packaged-water-aluminum-bottle/.

22. "Oliver Sacks, Casting Light on the Interconnectedness of Life," *New York Times*, August 30, 2015, https://www.nytimes.com/2015/08/31/arts/oliver-sacks-wrote-awakenings-and-cast-light-on-the-interconnectedness-of-life.html.

23. "Reassessing the Board Fight That Was Meant to Transform Exxon," *New York Times*, May 31, 2023, https://www.nytimes.com/2023/05/31/business/dealbook/engine-no-1-exxon-mobil.html.

24. "Steve Ballmer famously slammed the iPhone – here are 12 other times bosses got it wrong on new tech," *Business Insider*, June 29, 2017, https://www.businessinsider.com/iphone-steve-ballmer-bosses-mocked-new-technologyand-got-it-wrong-2017-6?r=US&IR=T.

25. "Future Readiness Insights," Hack Future Lab, November 2023.

26. "Corporate Sustainability Reporting Directive (CSRD) explained," Carbon Trust, December 15, 2022, https://www.carbontrust.com/news-and-insights/insights/corporate-sustainability-reporting-directive-csrd-explained.

27. "World is on the brink of catastrophic warming, U.N. climate change," *The Washington Post*, March 20, 2023, https://www.washingtonpost.com/climate-environment/2023/03/20/climate-change-ipcc-report-15/.

28. "Elon Musk sues OpenAI for abandoning original mission for profit," Reuters, March 1, 2024, https://www.reuters.com/legal/elon-musk-sues-openai-ceo-sam-altman-breach-contract-2024-03-01/.

29. "Gary Gensler urges regulators to tame AI risks to financial stability," *Financial Times*, October 15, 2023, https://www.ft.com/content/8227636f-e819-443a-aeba-c8237f0ec1ac.

30. "Top AI Experts Propose an International Panel on AI Safety," *Tech Times*, October 22, 2023, https://www.techtimes.com/articles/297839/20231022/pioneering-ai-experts-call-international-panel-ai-safety.htm.

31. "What Do Intelligent People Do Differently?" Medium Corporation Inc., November 23, 2023, https://medium.com/@bharatwater/what-do-intelligent-people-do-differently-ab4cedf592a0.

32. "Some reflections on the difference between 'Yes, but' and 'Yes, and,'" October 2020, https://transitionnetwork.org/news/yes-but-and-yes-and/.

33. "Nouriel Roubini warns of L-shaped 'Greater Depression,'" BNN Bloomberg, May 5, 2020, https://www.bnnbloomberg.ca/nouriel-roubini-warns-of-l-shaped-greater-depression-1.1431864.

34. "17 Successful Companies That Started Out During Crises," Zen Business, February 3, 2021, https://www.zenbusiness.com/blog/who-opened-in-crisis/.

35. "Future Readiness Insights," Hack Future Lab, November 2023.

36. "Lessons from Tesla's Approach to Innovation," by Nathan Furr and Jeff Dyer, *Harvard Business Review (HBR)*, February 12, 2020, https://hbr.org/2020/02/lessons-from-teslas-approach-to-innovation.

37. "Revolut invests in future growth as revenue tops $1bn in 2022; expects to hit $2bn in 2023," Revolut, https://www.revolut.com/en-NO/news/revolut_invests_in_future_growth_as_revenue_tops_1bn_in_2022_expects_to_hit_2bn_in_2023/.

38. "What's New in the 2023 Gartner Hype Cycle for Emerging Technologies," Gartner, August 23, 2023, https://www.gartner.com/en/articles/
what-s-new-in-the-2023-gartner-hype-cycle-for-emerging-technologies.
39. "Teaching Entrepreneurship – By Getting out of the Building," by Steve
Blank, March 11, 2010, https://steveblank.com/2010/03/11/teaching-
entrepreneurship-%E2%80%93-by-getting-out-of-the-building/.
40. "Future Readiness Insights," Hack Future Lab, November 2023.
41. "Better.com CEO fires 900 employees over Zoom," December 6, 2023,
CNN Business, https://edition.cnn.com/2021/12/05/business/better-ceo-
fires-employees/index.html.
42. "Future Readiness Insights," Hack Future Lab, November 2023.
43. "Yuval Noah Harari argues that AI has hacked the operating system of
human civilization," *The Economist*, April 28, 2023, https://www.economist
.com/by-invitation/2023/04/28/yuval-noah-harari-argues-that-ai-has-
hacked-the-operating-system-of-human-civilisation.
44. "Future Readiness Insights," Hack Future Lab, November 2023.
45. "Network effects: How to rebuild social capital and improve corporate performance," McKinsey & Company, August 2, 2022, https://www.mckinsey
.com/capabilities/people-and-organizational-performance/our-insights/
network-effects-how-to-rebuild-social-capital-and-improve-corporate-
performance.
46. "Microsoft CEO Satya Nadella: 10 Thoughts on the Post-COVID-19 World,"
San Antonio Summit, May 1, 2020, https://accelerationeconomy.com/cloud/
microsoft-ceo-satya-nadella-10-thoughts-on-the-post-covid-19-world/#.
47. "An Anthropological Gaze, Stories, and Reflections on NBIM culture,"
LinkedIn, February 4, 2024, https://www.linkedin.com/in/nicolai-tangen/
recent-activity/all/.
48. "How the World's Oldest Company Reinvented Itself" by Albrecht End-
ers and Lars Haggstrom, *Harvard Business Review (HBR)*, January 30,
2018, https://hbr.org/2018/01/how-the-worlds-oldest-company-reinvented-
itself.
49. "Future Readiness Insights," Hack Future Lab, November 2023.
50. "Meta shares dip is proof metaverse plan never really had legs," by Alex
Hern, *The Guardian*, October 27, 2022, https://www.theguardian.com/
technology/2022/oct/27/metas-shares-dip-is-proof-metaverse-plan-
never-really-had-legs-facebook.
51. "Future Readiness Insights," Hack Future Lab, November 2023.
52. "Future Readiness Insights," Hack Future Lab, November 2023.
53. "What Happened to Silicon Valley Bank," by Erin Gobbler, Investopedia,
February 27, 2024, https://www.investopedia.com/what-happened-to-
silicon-valley-bank-7368676.

Chapter 2

1. "*Black Mirror* Renewed for Season 7," *Variety*, November 21, 2023, https://variety.com/2023/tv/global/black-mirror-renewed-season-7-1235774423/.
2. "Adapting to AI: The New World of Organizational Ingenuity," by Josh Bersin, June 15, 2023, https://joshbersin.com/2023/06/adapting-to-ai-the-new-world-of-organizational-ingenuity/.
3. "AI Will Add $200 Trillion to the Economy by 2030," by Anthony Di Pizio, The Motley Fool, March 16, 2023, https://www.nasdaq.com/articles/ai-will-add-$200-trillion-to-the-economy-by-2030-says-ark-invest-2-socks-to-buy-if-it.
4. "Deep Work vs. Shallow Work with Cal Newport," Thinkers50, March 4, 2024, https://thinkers50.com/blog/work-and-life/deep-vs-shallow-work-cal-newport/.
5. "The Age of AI has begun," by Bill Gates, GatesNotes, The Blog of Bill Gates, March 21, 2023, https://www.gatesnotes.com/The-Age-of-AI-Has-Begun.
6. "Unlocking the Potential of AI Discovery," Wellcome Collection and BCG, March 1, 2024, https://cms.wellcome.org/sites/default/files/2023-06/unlocking-the-potential-of-AI-in-drug-discovery_report.pdf.
7. "What Sparked the Cambrian Explosion?" by Douglas Fox, *Scientific American*, February 16, 2016, https://www.scientificamerican.com/article/what-sparked-the-cambrian-explosion1/.
8. "Accounting Services Global Market Report," The Business Research Company, January 2024, https://www.thebusinessresearchcompany.com/report/accounting-services-global-market-report.
9. "The Global Automotive Industry is worth over $2.86 trillion," Nebula Investments, October 8, 2022, https://nebulainvestments.com/news/the-global-automotive-industry-is-worth-over-2-86-trillion/.
10. "Netflix Is Down 70%. Is It Time to Buy?" by Neil Patel, The Motley Fool, June 27, 2022, https://www.fool.com/investing/2022/06/27/netflix-is-down-70-is-it-time-to-buy/.
11. "Yesterday's Logic Speech," by Nathanael Benjamin, Executive Director of The Bank of England, July 3, 2023, https://www.bankofengland.co.uk/speech/2023/july/nathanael-benjamin-speech-at-uk-finance-pra-2023-supervisory-priorities-for-international-banks.
12. "Nvidia and other AI stocks are slumping. 'Amara's Law' explains why," by Alistair Bar, Yahoo! Finance, August 12, 2023, https://finance.yahoo.com/news/chart-ai-stocks-enter-correction-151922962.html.
13. "Generative AI to Become a $1.3 Trillion Market by 2032," Bloomberg, June 1, 2023, https://www.bloomberg.com/company/press/generative-ai-to-become-a-1-3-trillion-market-by-2032-research-finds/.

14. "AI could increase corporate profits by $4.4 trillion a year," McKinsey Global Institute, July 7, 2023, https://www.mckinsey.com/mgi/overview/in-the-news/ai-could-increase-corporate-profits-by-4-trillion-a-year-according-to-new-research.

15. "Corporate Ozempic," by Scott Galloway, No Mercy/No Malice, February 23, 2024, https://www.profgalloway.com/corporate-ozempic/.

16. "AI Will Transform the Global Economy. Let's Make Sure It Benefits Humanity," by Kristalina Georgieva, IMF Blog, January 14. 2024, https://www.imf.org/en/Blogs/Articles/2024/01/14/ai-will-transform-the-global-economy-lets-make-sure-it-benefits-humanity.

17. "The Reskilling Revolution," WEF, March 5, 2024, https://initiatives.weforum.org/reskilling-revolution/home.

18. "Make sure your brain has a diverse portfolio, too," *Financial Times*, by Gillian Tett, February 22, 2024, https://www.ft.com/content/e8a77da0-65fa-48b2-984f-15558a8e8700.

19. "Design for now, but with the future in mind: a 'cognitive flexibility theory' perspective on online learning through the lens of MOOCs," by Ying Hu and Rand J. Spiro, National Library of Medicine, January 8, 2021, https://www.ncbi.nlm.nih.gov/pmc/articles/PMC7793615/.

20. "William Gibson's Future Is Now," by Pagan Kennedy, *New York Times*, January 13, 2012, https://www.nytimes.com/2012/01/15/books/review/distrust-that-particular-flavor-by-william-gibson-book-review.html.

21. "Ada Lovelace and the Analytical Engine," by Christopher Hollings, Ursula Martin, and Adrian Rice, Oxford University, July 26, 2018, https://blogs.bodleian.ox.ac.uk/adalovelace/.

22. "ChatGPT sets record for fastest-growing user base - analyst note," by Krystal Hu, Reuters, February 2, 2023, https://www.reuters.com/technology/chatgpt-sets-record-fastest-growing-user-base-analyst-note-2023-02-01/.

23. "4 tech giants mentioned AI a total of 168 times on earnings calls, showing just how much attention the tech is attracting," by Jyoti Mann, *Business Insider*, April 30, 2023, https://www.businessinsider.com/tech-giants-mentioned-ai-168-times-on-earnings-calls-2023-4?r=US&IR=T.

24. "Disney Shuts Down Metaverse Unit as Part of First Wave of Layoffs," by Todd Spangler, *Variety*, March 28, 2023, https://variety.com/2023/digital/news/disney-shuts-down-metaverse-unit-layoffs-1235566501/.

25. "A majority of Americans have heard of ChatGPT, but few have tried it themselves," by Emily A. Vogels, Pew Research Center, May 24, 2023, https://www.pewresearch.org/short-reads/2023/05/24/a-majority-of-americans-have-heard-of-chatgpt-but-few-have-tried-it-themselves/.

26. "AI investment forecast to approach $200 billion globally by 2025," Goldman Sachs, August 1, 2024, https://www.goldmansachs.com/intelligence/pages/ai-investment-forecast-to-approach-200-billion-globally-by-2025.html.

27. "Future Readiness Insights," Hack Future Lab, November 2023.
28. "Organizations Form Alliance to Increase Tech Inclusion," by The Female Quotient, *AdAge*, December 17, 2021, https://adage.com/article/digital-marketing-ad-tech-news/global-interests-collaborate-boost-tech-diversity/2388506.
29. "Artificial Intelligence and the Future of Humans," by Nicolai Vassev, *Forbes*, May 6, 2021, https://www.forbes.com/sites/forbestechcouncil/2021/05/06/artificial-intelligence-and-the-future-of-humans/?sh=47ccf9e26e3b.
30. "Post Office scandal: key points from the latest court hearings," by Daniel Boffey and Mark Sweney, *The Guardian*, February 2, 2024, https://www.theguardian.com/uk-news/2024/feb/02/post-office-scandal-key-takeaways-latest-court-hearings.
31. "Cybercrime could cost 10.5 trillion dollars by 2025," by Shepard Smith, CNBC, March 9, 2021, https://www.cnbc.com/video/2021/03/09/cybercrime-could-cost-10-point-5-trillion-dollars-by-2025.html.
32. "NY Times sues OpenAI, Microsoft for infringing copyrighted works," by Jonathan Stempel, Reuters, December 27, 2023, https://www.reuters.com/legal/transactional/ny-times-sues-openai-microsoft-infringing-copyrighted-work-2023-12-27/.
33. "Mustafa Suleyman and Eric Schmidt: We need an AI equivalent of the IPCC," by Mustafa Suleyman and Eric Schmidt, *Financial Times*, October 19, 2023, https://www.ft.com/content/d84e91d0-ac74-4946-a21f-5f82eb4f1d2d.
34. "DPD AI chatbot swears, calls itself 'useless' and criticizes delivery firm," by Jane Clinton, *The Guardian*, January 20, 2024, https://www.theguardian.com/technology/2024/jan/20/dpd-ai-chatbot-swears-calls-itself-useless-and-criticises-firm.
35. "Future Readiness Insights," Hack Future Lab, November 2023.
36. "Surgeon General: We Have Become a Lonely Nation. It's Time to Fix That," by Vivek H. Murthy, April 30, 2023, https://www.nytimes.com/2023/04/30/opinion/loneliness-epidemic-america.html.
37. "WHO declares loneliness a 'global public health concern," by Sarah Johnson, *The Guardian*, November 16, 2023, https://www.theguardian.com/global-development/2023/nov/16/who-declares-loneliness-a-global-public-health-concern.
38. "The Big Con: How the Consulting Industry Undermines the State," by Sonja Hennen, Forum New Economy, July 13, 2023, https://newforum.org/en/short-cut-with-mariana-mazzucato-the-big-con/.
39. "The World's Oldest Populations," by Felix Richter, Statista, February 20, 2024, https://www.statista.com/chart/29345/countries-and-territories-with-the-highest-share-of-people-aged-65-and-older/.
40. "Drowning in Data, Starved for Information," by Eric D. Brown, October 22, 2014, https://ericbrown.com/drowning-in-data-starved-for-information.

41. "The Productivity Paradox," by Wickham Skinner, *Harvard Business Review*, July 1986, https://hbr.org/1986/07/the-productivity-paradox.
42. "What Is Human Nature? Paleolithic Emotions, Medieval Institutions, God-Like Technology," by Edward O. Wilson, Big Think, March 4, 2024, https://bigthink.com/hard-science/eo-wilson-what-makes-us-human-paleolithic-emotions-medieval-institutions-god-like-technology/.
43. "Do Less, Then Obsess. How to Work Smarter," by Emily Northway, Oslo Business Forum, June 13, 2019, https://www.obforum.com/article/morten-hansen-do-less-then-obsess.
44. "We're blind to our blindness. We have very little idea of how little we know. We're not designed to," by Daniel Kahneman, *The Independent*, November 24, 2011, https://www.independent.co.uk/arts-entertainment/books/features/we-re-blind-to-our-blindness-we-have-very-little-idea-of-how-little-we-know-we-re-not-designed-to-6267089.html.
45. "Growth mindsets and empathy are the reasons why Microsoft is back on top," by Nick Hobson, *Inc.*, January 16, 2024, https://www.inc.com/nick-hobson/satya-nadellas-microsoft-just-became-most-valued-company-in-world-its-thanks-to-psychology-not-tech.html.
46. "Designing Work That People Love," by Marcus Buckingham, *Harvard Business Review*, (May-June 2022), https://hbr.org/2022/05/designing-work-that-people-love.
47. "Gloat Announces Industry-First Talent Marketplace Ecosystem to Enable Complete Workforce Agility for Enterprises," Business Wire, September 29, 2021, https://www.businesswire.com/news/home/20210929005259/en/Gloat-Announces-Industry-First-Talent-Marketplace-Ecosystem-to-Enable-Complete-Workforce-Agility-for-Enterprises.
48. "Leadership Needs More Diversity and Less Supremacy," by Benjamin Laker, *Forbes*, March 2, 2020, https://www.forbes.com/sites/benjaminlaker/2020/03/02/leadership-needs-more-diversity-and-less-supremacy/.
49. "Future Readiness Insights," Hack Future Lab, November 2023.
50. "What a pixelated workforce means for your business," by Nicole Schreiber-Shearer, Gloat, February 26, 2024, https://gloat.com/blog/workforce-pixelation/.
51. "Future Readiness Insights," Hack Future Lab, November 2023.
52. "Live Long and Prosper," November 9, 2019, https://sbloom2.wordpress.com/2019/11/09/extinction-is-the-rule/.
53. "Accenture chief says most companies not ready for AI rollout," by Stephen Foley, *Financial Times*, November 19, 2023, https://www.ft.com/content/5d280f04-4aac-4295-8fb1-8571fab71046.
54. "To increase data skills, Airbnb has started its own university," by Bonnie Christian, *Wired UK*, July 12, 2017, https://www.wired.co.uk/article/airbnb-in-house-data-university-employee-skills.
55. "Future Readiness Insights," Hack Future Lab, November 2023.

56. "This Japanese concept will help you see the world – and learn – in a different way," by Kate Whiting, WEF, October 30, 2019, https://www .weforum.org/agenda/2019/10/japan-beginner-learning-shoshin/.

Chapter 3

1. "Fireside Chat with Terence Mauri and Amy C. Edmondson," Hack Future Lab, May 15, 2023, https://youtu.be/MXcvLu5Z6NI?si=3fxyH 9YeKvw3ktx_.
2. "Enshittification' is coming for absolutely everything," by Cory Doctorow, *Financial Times*, February 8, 2024, https://www.ft.com/content/6fb1602d -a08b-4a8c-bac0-047b7d64aba5.
3. "The Illiterate of the 21ˢᵗ Century . . ." by Eli Amdur, *Forbes*, October 4, 2022, https://www.forbes.com/sites/eliamdur/2022/10/04/the-illiterate- of-the-21st-century/.
4. "What is Half-Life of Knowledge," by John Spacey, Simplicable, Septem ber 25, 2016, https://simplicable.com/new/half-life-of-knowledge.
5. "Future Readiness Insights," Hack Future Lab, November 2023.
6. "San Francisco is understaffed by thousands. It takes eight months to hire one worker," by Joe Burn, *The San Francisco Standard*, June 22, 2023, https://sfstandard.com/2023/06/22/san-francisco-takes-255-days-to- hire-one-city-worker/.
7. "Take the Bureaucratic Mass Index (BMI) Survey," Humanocracy: Creat ing Organizations as Amazing as the People Inside Them," August 18, 2022, https://www.humanocracy.com/course/BMI.
8. "Future Readiness Insights," Hack Future Lab, November 2023.
9. "Pentagon buries evidence of $125 billion in bureaucratic waste," by Craig Whitlock and Bob Woodward, *The Washington Post*, December 5, 2016, https://www.washingtonpost.com/investigations/pentagon-bur ies-evidence-of-125-billion-in-bureaucratic-waste/2016/12/05/ e0668c76-9af6-11e6-a0ed-ab0774c1eaa5_story.html.
10. "Meta's 'Year of Efficiency' was everything Wall Street needed to hear from Zuckerberg," by Jonathan Vanian, CNBC, February 1, 2023, https:// www.cnbc.com/2023/02/01/metas-year-of-efficiency-everything-wall- street-needed-to-hear.html.
11. "Fail quickly and inexpensively: Nvidia founder and CEO Jensen Huang shares his mantra for success," by Jing Pang, Yahoo! Finance, February 27, 2024, https://uk.finance.yahoo.com/news/fail-quickly-inexpensively-nvidia- founder-130300123.html#.
12. "Failure Found to Be an Essential Prerequisite for Success," by David Noonan, *Scientific American*, October 30, 2019, https://www.scientifi camerican.com/article/failure-found-to-be-an-essential-prerequisite-

for-success/?utm_source=nomercynomalice.beehiiv.com&utm_medium =newsletter&utm_campaign=quitting-time.

13. "Future Readiness Insights," Hack Future Lab, November 2023.

14. "How Amazon CEO Jeff Bezos has inspired people to change the way they think about failure," by Eugene Kim, *Business Insider*, May 28, 2016, https://www.businessinsider.com/how-amazon-ceo-jeff-bezos-thinks-about-failure-2016-5?r=US&IR=T.

15. "Central banks rethink forecasting after failures on inflation," by Sam Fleming, Martin Arnold, and Colby Smith, *Financial Times*, December 28, 2023, https://www.ft.com/content/5d7851f3-ef7c-4599-8a5c-c34cecb83511.

16. "How Failure Breeds Success: The Deliberate Amateur," by Sarah Lewis, *Slate*, May 21, 2014, https://slate.com/business/2014/05/nobel-prize-in-physics-andre-geim-went-from-levitating-frogs-to-sciences-highest-honor.html.

17. "Designed by clowns': Boeing messages raise serious questions about 737 Max," by Gwyn Topham, *The Guardian*, January 10, 2020, https://www.theguardian.com/business/2020/jan/09/boeing-737-max-internal-messages.

18. "The man who studies the spread of ignorance," by Georgina Kenyon, BBC Future, January 6, 2016, https://www.bbc.com/future/article/20160105-the-man-who-studies-the-spread-of-ignorance.

19. "Leaked Documents Show How Uber Embraced Violence to Achieve Its Corporate Ambitions," by Courtney Vinopal, Observer, November 7, 2022, https://observer.com/2022/07/leaked-documents-show-how-uber-embraced-violence-to-achieve-its-corporate-ambitions/.

20. "Uber Files: Greyballing, kill switches, lobbying – Uber's dark tricks revealed," by Nassos Stylianou, Becky Dale, and Will Dahlgreen, BBC News, July 11, 2022, https://www.bbc.co.uk/news/resources/idt-f2971465-73d2-4932-a889-5c63778e273d.

21. "Big Four Accounting Firms Come Under Regulator's Scrutiny," by Dave Michaels, *The Washington Post* March 15, 2022, https://www.wsj.com/articles/big-four-accounting-firms-come-under-regulators-scrutiny-11647364574.

22. "Inside Uber's Effort To Fix Its Culture Through a Harvard-Inspired 'University,'" by Biz Carson, *Forbes*, February 3, 2018, https://www.forbes.com/sites/bizcarson/2018/02/03/inside-ubers-effort-to-fix-its-culture-through-a-harvard-inspired-university/?sh=2bd333bc1695.

23. "Uber hires Harvard Business School professor to overhaul culture," by Hannah Kuchler, *Financial Times*, June 5, 2017, https://www.ft.com/content/58c73f56-4a30-11e7-919a-1e14ce4af89b.

24. "CEOs forced to ditch decades of forecasting habits," by Anne-Sylvaine Chassany, *Financial Times*, February 16, 2023, https://www.ft.com/content/456baa69-83df-4c7f-af7b-49e6451a1183.

25. "Future Readiness Insights," Hack Future Lab, November 2023.
26. "Work Shift: How Shopify Culled 320,000 Hours of Meetings," by Matthew Boyle, Bloomberg UK, February 14, 2023, https://www .bloomberg.com/news/newsletters/2023-02-14/how-shopify-cut-320-000-hours-of-unnecessary-meetings?embedded-checkout=true.
27. "Future Readiness Insights," Hack Future Lab, November 2023.
28. "The time has come to start playing to win," by Timo Mansikka-aho, Nordic Business Report, May 17, 2022, https://www.nbforum.com/nbre port/the-time-has-come-to-start-playing-to-win/.
29. "New research shows what NASA can teach organizations about strategic agility," by Kim Matthies, Phys Org, November 30, 2023, https://phys .org/news/2023-11-nasa-strategic-agility.html.
30. "How 100 VC Rejections Led to a $26 Billion Startup for This 35-Year-Old," by Caleb Naysmith, Yahoo! Finance, June 16, 2023, https://finance .yahoo.com/news/100-vc-rejections-led-26-150012207.html.
31. "New Bayer CEO Bill Anderson's move to cut management mirrors his Roche playbook," by Brian Buntz, Pharmaceutical Processing World, September 18, 2023, https://www.pharmaceuticalprocessingworld.com/ bayer-ceo-bill-anderson-roche-strategy/.

Chapter 4

1. "Future Readiness Insights," Hack Future Lab, November 2023.
2. "Microsoft hits $3 trillion market value, second to Apple," by Chibuike Oguh, January 25, 2024, https://www.reuters.com/technology/microsoft-hits-3-trillion-market-value-2024-01-24/.
3. "Choosing to grow: The leader's blueprint," McKinsey & Company, July 7, 2022, https://www.mckinsey.com/capabilities/growth-marketing-and-sales/our-insights/choosing-to-grow-the-leaders-blueprint.
4. "Gary Hame: Can Big Firms Be Agile?" by Steve Denning, *Forbes*, November 26, 2016, https://www.forbes.com/sites/stevedenning/2016/11/27/ gary-hamel-can-big-firms-be-agile/?sh=66ddb5b838c5.
5. "Joseph Schumpeter's gales of creative destruction," by Mark Dodgson and David Gann, Oxford Academic, August 2018, https://academic.oup .com/book/447/chapter-abstract/135232560?redirectedFrom=fulltext.
6. "John Deere, Inventor," March 1, 2024, Wikipedia, https://en.wikipedia .org/wiki/John_Deere_(inventor).
7. "John Deere among 100 best global brands," by Profi Team, *The Farm Machinery Magazine*, November 19, 2018, https://www.profi.co.uk/news/ john-deere-among-100-best-global-brands/.

8. "The Rise and Fall of General Electric (GE)," by Sarah Hansen, Investopedia, January 11, 2024, https://www.investopedia.com/insights/rise-and-fall-ge/.

9. "Credit Suisse's Fate Was Sealed by Regulators Days Before UBS Deal," by Marion Halftermeyer, Dinesh Nair, Abhinav Ramnarayan, Jan-Henrik Foerster, and Gillian Tan, Bloomberg UK, March 20, 2023, https://www.bloomberg.com/news/features/2023-03-20/credit-suisse-ubs-takeover-how-a-166-year-old-bank-collapsed?leadSource=uverify%20wall.

10. "A new technology boom is at hand," by Rana Foroohar, *Financial Times*, March 27, 2023, https://www.ft.com/content/cb7391b2-5d17-4806-b05c-c6125129264c.

11. "A new technology boom is at hand," by Rana Foroohar, *Financial Times*, March 27, 2023, https://www.ft.com/content/cb7391b2-5d17-4806-b05c-c6125129264c.

12. "Future Readiness Insights," Hack Future Lab, November 2023.

13. "AstraZeneca: Scaling Simplification," by Hayagreeva Rao, Julie Makinen, Case Study, Stanford Graduate School of Business, 2017, https://www.gsb.stanford.edu/faculty-research/case-studies/astrazeneca-scaling-simplification.

14. "Future Readiness Insights," Hack Future Lab, November 2023.

15. "Keep it simple, scientists: AZ's productivity push regains 1 million hours," by Linda Banks, PharmaPhorum, October 11, 2017, https://pharmaphorum.com/views-and-analysis/az-time-management-productivity-push.

16. "Emissions by sector: where do greenhouse gases come from?" by Hannah Ritchie, Pablo Rosado, and Max Roser, Our World in Data, January 2024, https://ourworldindata.org/emissions-by-sector.

17. "Taylor Swift," by Adrienne Donica, Biography.com, February 5, 2024, https://www.biography.com/musicians/taylor-swift.

18. "Taylor Swift's The Eras Tour Could Generate $4.6 Billion for Local Economies," by Hugh McIntyre, https://www.forbes.com/sites/hughmcintyre/2023/06/09/taylor-swifts-the-eras-tour-could-generate-46-billion-for-local-economies/?sh=71fcd69d442d.

19. "Future Readiness Insights," Hack Future Lab, November 2023.

20. "Case study: Patagonia's 'Don't buy this jacket' campaign," by Josei Allchin, Marketing Week, January 23, 2013, https://www.marketingweek.com/case-study-patagonias-dont-buy-this-jacket-campaign/.

21. "Patagonia's billionaire owner gives away the company to fight the climate crisis," by Erin McCormick, *The Guardian*, September 15, https://www.theguardian.com/us-news/2022/sep/14/patagonias-billionaire-owner-gives-away-company-to-fight-climate-crisis-yvon-chouinard.

22. "Climate change: IPCC report is 'code red for humanity,'" by Matt McGrath, BBC News, August 9, 2021, https://www.bbc.co.uk/news/science-environment-58130705.

23. "WWF Living Planet Report: Devastating 69% drop in wildlife populations since 1970," WWF, October 13, 2022, https://www.wwf.eu/?7780966/WWF-Living-Planet-Report-Devastating-69-drop-in-wildlife-populations-since-1970.

24. "Patagonia's founder just donated the entire company, worth $3 billion, to fight climate change," by Lora Kolodny, CNBC, September 14, 2022, https://www.cnbc.com/2022/09/14/patagonia-founder-donates-entire-company-to-fight-climate-change.html.

25. "Milton Friedman's wisdom endures: companies should be run for shareholders," by Steve Kaplan, Economist Impact, June 21, 2022, https://impact.economist.com/sustainability/circular-economies/milton-friedmans-wisdom-endures-companies-should-be-run-for-shareholders/.

26. "Our Beginnings," by Allbirds, March 4, 2024, https://www.allbirds.co.uk/pages/sustainable-practices#beginnings.

27. "Patagonia's billionaire owner gives away the company to fight the climate crisis," by Erin McCormick, *The Guardian*, September 15, 2022, https://www.theguardian.com/us-news/2022/sep/14/patagonias-billionaire-owner-gives-away-company-to-fight-climate-crisis-yvon-chouinard.

28. "Breaking the tragedy of the horizon – climate change and financial stability – speech by Mark Carney," Bank of England, September 29, 2015, https://www.bankofengland.co.uk/speech/2015/breaking-the-tragedy-of-the-horizon-climate-change-and-financial-stability.

29. "Global Economic Uncertainty Remains Elevated, Weighing on Growth." by Hites Ahir, Nicholas Bloom, Davide Furceri, IMF Blog, January 26, 2023, https://www.imf.org/en/Blogs/Articles/2023/01/26/global-economic-uncertainty-remains-elevated-weighing-on-growth.

30. "History Repeats, and It Doesn't," Daily Stoic, February 4, https://dailystoic.com/history-repeats-and-it-doesnt/.

31. "From Polycrisis to Permacrisis," by Erik Assadourian, Resilience, January2023,https://www.resilience.org/stories/2023-01-03/from-polycrisis-to-permacrisis/.

32. "Anomalies Wanted: A counterintuitive call to innovate that can set the business apart," by Esther Clark, The Christensen Institute, March 23,2023,https://www.christenseninstitute.org/blog/anomalies-wanted-a-counterintuitive-call-to-innovate-that-can-set-businesses-apart/.

33. "Instagram Was First Called 'Burbn,'" by Megan Garber, *The Atlantic*, July 2, 2014, https://www.theatlantic.com/technology/archive/2014/07/instagram-used-to-be-called-brbn/373815/.

34. "Beyonder Creativity," by Mindtools, March 4, 2024, https://www.mindtools.com/ayousci/beyonder-creativity.

35. "From fossil fuels to renewables – within a decade: key lessons from Ørsted's green transformation," by Jakob Askou Boss, Climate Champions, June 22, 2021, https://racetozero.unfccc.int/from-fossil-fuels-to-renewables-within-a-decade-key-lessons-from-orsteds-green-transformation-2/.

36. "From fossil fuels to green energy: the Ørsted story," by Rob Morris, London Business School, July 2, 2018, https://www.london.edu/think/iie-from-fossil-fuels-to-green-energy-the-orsted-story.

37. "The Top 20 Business Transformations of the Last Decade," by Scott D. Anthony, Alasdair Trotter, and Evan I. Schwartz, HBR, September 24, 2019, https://hbr.org/2019/09/the-top-20-business-transformations-of-the-last-decade.

38. "Future Readiness Insights," Hack Future Lab, November 2023.

39. "Can We Get Anywhere Without Thought?" by David Bohm, What Is Dialogue Blog, March 4, 2024, https://www.whatisdialogue.com/tag/david-bohm/.

40. "The Essential John le Carré," by Sam Adler-Bell, *New York Times*, July 13, 2023, https://www.nytimes.com/article/john-le-carre-books.html.

41. "Mudita," Wikipedia, February 4, 2024, https://en.wikipedia.org/wiki/Mudita.

Chapter 5

1. "People trust businesses more than governments with new tech like AI, but they're still wary," by Eamon Barrett, *Fortune*, January 19, 2024, https://fortune.com/2024/01/19/edelman-annual-barometer-public-trust-in-businesses-and-institutions/.

2. "How to rebuild trust in institutions: results, results, results," by Lord Mark Malloch-Brown, WEF, December 18, 2023, https://www.weforum.org/agenda/2023/12/how-to-rebuild-trust-in-philanthropy-results-results-results/.

3. "Future Readiness Insights," Hack Future Lab, November 2023.

4. "Future Readiness Insights," Hack Future Lab, November 2023.

5. "Future Readiness Insights," Hack Future Lab, November 2023.

6. "Does your organization have productivity paranoia?" by Nicole Schreiber-Shearer, Gloat, January 11, 2024, https://gloat.com/blog/skills-intelligence-tools-productivity/.

7. "Future Readiness Insights," Hack Future Lab, November 2023.

8. "After CVS Stopped Cigarette Sales, Smokers Stopped Buying Elsewhere, Too," by Bruce Japsen, *Forbes*, February 20, 2017, https://www.forbes.com/sites/brucejapsen/2017/02/20/after-cvs-stopped-cigarette-sales-smokers-stopped-buying-elsewhere-too/.

9. "Future Readiness Insights," Hack Future Lab, November 2023.
10. "The trust crisis: Facebook, Boeing, and many other firms are losing the public's faith. Can they regain it?" by Sandra J. Sucher and Shalene Gupta, HBR, July 18, 2019, http://www.circulodedirectores.org/2019/07/18/the-trust-crisis-facebook-boeing-and-too-many-other-firms-are-losing-the-publics-faith-can-they-regain-it/.
11. "Spending on digital transformation technologies and services worldwide from 2017 to 2026," by Ahmed Sherif, Statista, August 6, 2023, https://www.statista.com/statistics/870924/worldwide-digital-transformation-market-size/.
12. "Future Readiness Insights," Hack Future Lab, November 2023.
13. "The Librarian's Catch-22: Understanding Vocational Awe and Its Stereotypes," by Sarah Lee, GR Tech, June 16, 2023, https://www.grtech.com/blog/understanding-vocational-awe.
14. "Future Readiness Insights," Hack Future Lab, November 2023.
15. "Establish a performance culture as your secret sauce," by Brooke Wed dle, Ran Li Phelps, and Alexander DiLeonardo, McKinsey & Company, July 27, 2020, https://www.mckinsey.com/capabilities/people-and-organizational-performance/our-insights/the-organization-blog/establish-a-performance-culture-as-your-secret-sauce.
16. "A Few of the Unique Sensors Used in Formula 1," by Formula Bharat, 5 March 2022, https://www.formulabharat.com/blog/a-few-of-the-unique-sensors-used-in-formula-1/.
17. "House museums #55: the Eames House," by Anne Wallentine, *Financial Times*, February 17, 2024, https://www.ft.com/content/fe2120b3-5cc0-4809-9f60-aeede8c283ee.
18. "Future Readiness Insights," Hack Future Lab, November 2023.
19. "Lynda Gratton interview with Terence Mauri," Hack The Future podcast, September 22, 2022, https://open.spotify.com/episode/7FOLHWYwQxvBQxb4UBNDYA?si=iYlRLQUtT2yyNa8xifd_4w.
20. "Future Readiness Insights," Hack Future Lab, November 2023.
21. "Future Readiness Insights," Hack Future Lab, November 2023.
22. "Barack Obama's Working Is a Timely Reality Check on the American Dream – Until It Gets to the Bosses," by Judy Berman, *Time Magazine*, May 17, 2023, https://time.com/6279943/working-review-obama-netflix/.
23. "*Working* (Terkel book)," Wikipedia, March 4, 2024, https://en.wikipedia.org/wiki/Working_(Terkel_book).
24. "Unilever releases financial results of Compass Organization overhaul," by Carla Seipp, Beauty Matter, October 23, 2022, https://beautymatter.com/articles/unilever-releases-financial-results-of-compass-organisation-overhaul.
25. "Future Readiness Insights," Hack Future Lab, November 2023.

26. "Google CEO tells employees productivity and focus must improve, launches 'Simplicity Sprint' to gather employee feedback on efficiency," by Jennifer Elias, CNBC, July 31, 2022, https://www.cnbc.com/2022/07/31/ google-ceo-to-employees-productivity-and-focus-must-improve .html#:~:text=Google%20is%20launching%20a%20new,during%20 an%20uncertain%20economic%20environment.

27. "Google must get better at 'dog-fooding,' says search quality chief," by Josh Halliday, *The Guardian*, September 30, 2011, https://www.theguardian .com/technology/pda/2011/sep/30/google-dog-fooding-search-quality.

28. "Future Readiness Insights," Hack Future Lab, November 2023.

29. "Wake up to the new workplace evolution," by Gary Hamel and Stefan Stern, Think at London Business School, July 15, 2020, https://www .london.edu/think/wake-up-to-the-new-workplace-revolution.

30. "Fixing bureaucracy requires more than a month-long sprint. Here's why," by Gary Hamel and Michele Zanini, Fast Company, September 16, 2022,https://www.fastcompany.com/90789977/fixing-bureaucracy-requires- more-than-a-month-long-sprint-heres-why.

31. "He steered a big comeback at Puma. Could Bjørn Gulden do the same for Adidas?" by Madeleine Schulz and Maliha Shoaib, Vogue Business, November 7, 2022, https://www.voguebusiness.com/companies/he- steered-a-big-comeback-at-puma-could-bjorn-gulden-do-the-same- for-adidas.

32. "Overconsumption in the fashion industry," by Richard Vasquez Jr, Fashion Revolution, March 3, 2022, https://www.fashionrevolution.org/ overconsumption-in-the-fashion-industry/.

33. "Hermès creates a mycelium version of its classic leather Victoria bag," by Jennifer Hahn, Dezeen, March 18, 2021, https://www.dezeen .com/2021/03/18/hermes-mycelium-leather-victoria-bag-mycoworks/.

34. "Sustainable fashion: Biomaterial revolution replacing fur and skins," by Jennifer Gonzales, Mongabay, April 8, 2022, https://news.mongabay .com/2022/04/sustainable-fashion-biomaterial-revolution-replacing- fur-and-skins/.

35. "Get rid of the 'feedback sandwich' – use this one sentence instead, says Wharton psychologist Adam Grant," by Ece Yildirim, CNBC, December 13, 2023, https://www.cnbc.com/2023/12/13/adam-grant-feedback- sandwiches-dont-work-use-this-sentence-instead.html.

36. "Unleash the power of our people," Pfizer 2019 Annual Review, https://www .pfizer.com/sites/default/files/investors/financial_reports/ annual_reports/2019/our-bold-moves/unleash-the-power-of-our-people/ index.html.

37. "Future Readiness Insights," Hack Future Lab, November 2023.

38. "Jamie Dimon's 'listening' bus? Get on board," by Gillian Tett, *Financial Times*,August15,2018,https://www.ft.com/content/693890ca-a019-11e8-85da-eeb7a9ce36e4.

39. "In 2023, women CEOs finally outnumbered CEOs named John," by Gabriela Huerta, *CEO Magazine*, March 8, 2024, https://www.theceo magazine.com/business/management-leadership/countries-with-the-most-female-ceos/.

40. "Future Readiness Insights," Hack Future Lab, November 2023.

41. "Future Readiness Insights," Hack Future Lab, November 2023.

42. "Accenture Ranked No.1 on Refinitiv Index of World's Most Diverse and Inclusive Companies," Accenture Newsroom, September 29, 2022, https://newsroom.accenture.com/news/2022/accenture-ranked-no-1-on-refinitiv-index-of-worlds-most-diverse-and-inclusive-companies#:~:text=NEW%20YORK%3B%20Sept.,and%20governance%20(ESG)%20data.

43. Future Readiness Insights," Hack Future Lab, November 2023.

44. "More than a third of world's population have never used the internet, says UN," by *The Guardian*, March 4, 2024, https://www.theguardian.com/technology/2021/nov/30/more-than-a-third-of-worlds-population-has-never-used-the-internet-says-un.

Chapter 6

1. Future Readiness Insights," Hack Future Lab, November 2023.

2. "Starbucks unveils plan to add 17,000 locations by 2030, cut $3 billion in costs," by Amelia Lucas, CNBC, November 2, 2023, https://www.cnbc.com/2023/11/02/starbucks-unveils-expansion-plans-cost-cutting.html.

3. "What Is Moore's Law and Is It Still True?" by Carla Tardi, Investopedia, February 11, 2024, https://www.investopedia.com/terms/m/mooreslaw.asp.

4. "Beware the 'botshit': why generative AI is such a real and imminent threat to the way we live," by André Spicer, *The Guardian*, January 3, 2024, https://www.theguardian.com/commentisfree/2024/jan/03/botshit-generative-ai-imminent-threat-democracy.

5. "How Many Emails Are Sent Per Day (New Data)," by Rohit Shewale, DemandSage, March 1, 2023, https://www.demandsage.com/how-many-emails-are-sent-per-day/.

6. "The Attention Economy," by Lexie Kane, Nielsen Norman Group, June 30, 2019, https://www.nngroup.com/articles/attention-economy/.

7. "The Next Revolution," Think Different, December 1, 2012, https://flowchainsensei.wordpress.com/2012/12/01/the-next-revolution/.

8. Future Readiness Insights," Hack Future Lab, November 2023.

9. "NIKE, Inc. Sets Bold Vision and Targets for 2020," Business Wire, May 11, 2016, https://www.businesswire.com/news/home/20160511005885/ en/NIKE-Inc.-Sets-Bold-Vision-and-Targets-for-2020.

10. "Remember When Yahoo Turned Down $1 Million to Buy Google?" by Jason Derrick, Yahoo Finance, July 25, 2016, https://finance.yahoo.com/ news/remember-yahoo-turned-down-1-132805083.html.

11. "Searching for Trouble," Ken Auletta, *The New Yorker*, October 5, 2009, https://www.newyorker.com/magazine/2009/10/12/searching-for-trouble.

12. "Verizon Announces $4.8 Billion Deal for Yahoo's Internet Business," by Vindu Goel, *The New York Times*, July 25, 2016, https://www.nytimes .com/2016/07/26/business/verizon-yahoo-sale.html.

13. "Forget Dieselgate – a bigger emissions problem hides in plain sight," by Nick Molden, *Financial Times*, October 30, 2023, https://www.ft.com/ content/5a282b2e-1d75-4ed4-a69e-289d858eb6ee.

14. "The rise and fall of Sears is the perfect symbol of retail's challenges over the last decade," by Áine Cain, Business Insider, December 11, 2019, https://www.businessinsider.com/sears-rise-fall-retail-world-last-decade-2019-12?r=US&IR=T.

15. "How SpaceX Keeps Its Startup Culture," by Gwynne Shotwell, *Forbes*, February 7, 2014, https://www.forbes.com/sites/women2/2014/02/07/ gwynne-shotwell-how-spacex-keeps-its-startup-culture/?sh=4369f26631d9.

16. "How examining our regrets can make for a more meaningful life," by Elise Hu and Andee Tagle, NPR, December 21, 2022, https://www.npr .org/2022/03/16/1087010308/the-power-of-regret-how-examining-regret-can-help-you-live-a-meaningful-life.

17. "The Lost Generation and the Writers Who Described Their World," by Robert Longley, ThoughtCo., March 2, 2022, https://www.thoughtco .com/the-lost-generation-4159302.

Acknowledgments

Many exceptional individuals, clients, friends, and mentors have inspired me to write *The Upside of Disruption*. Thank you to my editorial team at Wiley, Neill Brian, Deborah Schindlar, Gabriela Mancuso, and Jesse Wiley. Thank you to the global leadership community who supported me, especially the Co-founders of Thinkers50, Stuart Crainer and Des Dearlove, Richard Straub, Astrid Groborsch, and Simon Caulkin at The Global Peter Drucker Forum, Nordic Business Forum, Harvard Business School, Dave Ulrich, Rensis Likert Professor, Ross School of Business University of Michigan Partner, The RBL Group, Anders Dons, Nordic CEO, Deloitte; Mette Schoennemann, Deloitte; Mark Fortier, CEO of Fortier PR; Professor Amy Edmondson, Tahirou Assane and Emil Andersson at The Brightline Project Management Institute; Alex Amouyel, the former Executive Director at MIT Solve; Yannick Theler, CEO of Steer Studios; Julia Hobshawm, OBE; Dan Cable, author of *Alive at Work: The Neuroscience of Helping Your People Love What They Do*; Abigail Posner, Director, Creative Works at Google; Michele Zanini, co-author of *Humanocracy*; Frank-Jürgen Richter, Founder and Chairman, Horasis; Chris Barton, Founder of Shazam; Derek Sweeney, Founder of The Sweeney Agency; Steve Hamilton, Partner & Chief Coaching Officer, The Henka Institute; Aalim Mohamed, Founder of the World of Tomorrow Summit; Katja Schipperheijn, Founder of Habit

Improvement; Grace Chen, Quantic School of Business and Technology; Friederike Fabritius, Neuroscientist and author; Monica Neacsu; Greg Satell, Co-founder of ChangeOS and Wharton Business School lecturer; Kaihan Krippendorg, CEO of Outhinker Networks; Dr. Rebecca Heiss, CEO and Founder of Icueity; Dainius Baltrusaitis, CEO and Founder of Confinn Europe; Tomas Chamorro-Premuzic, Professor of Business Psychology at UCL and Columbia; Scott Newton, Managing Partner, Thinking Dimensions; Artur Smejlis, Founder of Everyday Development; Samuel West, Founder of the Museum of Failure; Peter Fisk, Academic Director of IE Business School and Founder of GeniusWorks; Mirjana Novkovic, Jan Madura, Danielle Sweeney, Rick Gimea; Paolo Gallo, author, and former Chief Human Resources Officer at the World Economic Forum; Benjamin Laker, author and Professor of Leadership and Director of Impact and Global Engagement at Henley Business School; Rachel Treece, CEO, Henka Institute; Jon Brix, Pia Hinz, and Henrik Poulsen at A-Speakers; Dan Pontefract, Thinkers50 Radar and author of *Work-Life Bloom*; E. Elisabet Lahti, Ph.D., Founder of Sisu Lab, author of *Gentle Power: A Revolution in How We Think, Lead and Succeed Using the Finnish Art of Sisu*; Monique Borst, CEO, catalyst, strategist, and coach; Marga Hoek, author of *Tech For Good: Solving The World's Greatest Challenges*; Cosimo Turroturro, Eric Pepin, William Welch, Frances Welch, Nello and Rita Mauri, Sonia and Lucia Mauri, Eileen Mauri, Tom Gregory, Matt Ryder, Luka Pirnat, London Speakers Bureau, A-Speakers, Raise The Bar, Executive Speakers, Alex Moore, Genaro Rino Mugnano, Byron and Allie Cloete Welch, David Lancefield, Loida Perel, Monika Kosman, Susanna Hagelstam, Chris Teague, Natasha Darcy Souza and Paul Lister.

Finally, I want to thank my partner, Polona Pirnat, for her patience and support throughout this project's countless hours, evenings, and weekends.

About the Author

Thinkers50, the global ranking authority of the top management thinkers, has described Terence Mauri as "an influential and outspoken thinker on the future of leadership." He founded the management think tank Hack Future Lab and is a visiting professor at some of the world's leading business schools, where he partners with organizations to sharpen their future readiness. Terence speaks to leadership teams about how to lead the future boldly for firms and institutions worldwide, including Google, Pfizer, Assurant, Unilever, HSBC, and MIT. His thinking has been featured in Forbes, Inc., The Economist, BBC News, Strategy + Business, and the Global Peter Drucker Forum.

Index

A

Activation (bureaucratic BS counterstrategy), 77–78
Age of AI, 16, 45, 52, 61, 165
Age of Co-Intelligence, 8, 23–24, 63
Age of Wonder, 33
Agility, 24–25, 67, 149
  gap, attention, 71–74
  mental tools, 93–94
Airbnb, data/analytics culture, 62
Algorithmic Society, rise, 38
Altman, Sam, 4
Amara's Law, 39–40
Amazonification
  disruptive forces, 37–38
  principles, 38–39
Analytical Machine, proposal, 42–43
Angelou, Maya, 105
Animal Farm (Orwell), 139
Annual trust barometer (Edelman), 136
"Anomalies Welcome," 121–122
Anxiety, 24
Anything Workforce, 55–60
App economy, evolution/change, 110
Armstrong, Jesse, 171
Artificial intelligence (AI), 17
  adoption, phases, 42–43
  AI-driven disruption, 5, 23

AI-powered talent marketplace, soft launch, 60
black swan event, 46
building, 13
chatbot, DPD cessation, 47
code red, 36–39
co-thinker role, 36
disruption, 40–41, 58
embracing, 40–41
evolution, 46–47
founding, 43
future, 41, 60–61
  readiness, 34
harnessing, 57
history, 42–47
impact, 5–6
  warning, 60
intelligence illusion, 47–50
leadership/humanity, matching, 54–55
leveraging, 8
meaning, 63
revolution, 36, 115
risk, relationship, 39–40
success, 13–14
technologies, investment, 44
value generation, 40
warning signal, 50
Astra Zeneco, simplification drive (usage), 112

Attention
  clarifier role, 52
  poverty, 175
  types, 53–54
Automated self-checkouts, 48
Avoid-failure mindset, 84

B
Babbage, Charles, 42–43
Back-to-back meetings, increase, 52
Ballmer, Steve, 12
Bankman Fried, Sam, 141
Becoming, 148
Believing, 146
Belonging, 146–147
Best practices, 71–72
Beyonders, 122–125
  cultures, 126
  movement, igniting, 125
Bezos, Jeff, 82
Billion-dollar beliefs, 118–119
Black Mirror (TV series), 33
Blank, Steve, 21
Blockchain, convergence, 17–18
Boeing MAX 737 crisis, 85–86
Boldness
  demands, 106–107
  meaning, 181
Bonding, Belonging, and Becoming
  (Three Bs), 12
Braving, 147
Bring your own divergence
  (BYOD), 162–164
British Post Office, scandal, 141
Broken practices, 72
Bronze Age, 16
Bureaucratic activities, scheduling, 76
Bureaucratic BS, 73
  acknowledgment, 77
  counterstrategies, 77–79
  measurement, 75
  occurrence, 76
Bureaucratic bullshit (BS), 72–76

Bureaucratic Mass index, 73
Burnout, suffering, 55
Business disruption, 5
Business models/cultures, 145
Buurtzorg
  decision-making deceleration/
    trust erosion, 152
  How We Work
    dimension, 152–153
ByteDance, 38

C
Cambrian Explosion, drivers, 36–37
Capitalism, reimagining, 117–118
Care, Commitment, Contribution,
    and Co-creation (4Cs), 164
Career ladder, 57
Carney, Mark, 119
Certainty, anticipation, 176
Cessario, Mike, 11–12
Challenger Trust, 71
Change
  adaptation, ability, 70–71
  challenge, 104
  willingness/humility, 15–16
Character skills, 55
Chat checkouts, support, 47–48
ChatGPT (OpenAI), 13, 43
  benefits, 28
Chouinard, Yvon, 116–118
Christensen, Clayton, 121–122
Circumstances, change
    (adaptation), 68
Clarke, Arthur C., 33
Cognitive burnout, suffering, 55
Cognitive diversity, 163
Cognitive flexibility, 41–42
Cognitive shock, 7
Cognitive skills, 55
Cognitive underload, 55
Co-lab, 18
Cold technology, 48–49
Collaboration, support, 44

Collective future blindness, 5
Collective mindset, cultivation, 15–16
Collective trust, 20
Comfort zone, 106
Companies, long-term vitality
     (risks), 103–104
Compass Organization, launch, 151
Competitive advantage, half-life, 69
Competitors, impact, 12
Complexity
   burden, 156
   creation, success
      (impact), 137–138
   fight, simplicity (usage), 52
   reduction, 78, 111
Conformity, cultures, 38
Consultification, 48
Consumer Electronics Show (CES),
     event, 103
Control/efficiency, prioritization, 5
Corporate Sustainability Reporting
     Directive, 13
Cost constraints, 5
Counterfactual thinking,
     strength, 111
Counter-intuitive decision, 48
Courage, 108–115
   advantage, 26–27, 107
   dividend, 108
   impact, 3
   importance, 104–105
   leaders of courage, 127
   OKRs, 126
   return on courage, 112–115
   skills, new leadership, 175–177
Criticism, problems, 159
Cross-disciplinary thinking, 56
Cross-industry synergies, value, 9
Cultural diversity, 163
Culture
   toxic culture, unlearning, 87–91
   unlearning, 91
Customers, 10–12

D
Data, Agility, Risk, and Evolution
     (DARE), 22–23, 29–30
   Leadership Test, 189–190
Data, AI speed, 23–24, 33
Decarbonization, 13, 15–16,
     27, 35, 110
   leadership, 124–125
   opportunity, 126
   revolution, 121
Decision loops, acceleration/
     reduction, 107
Decision-making, stength, 112
Deepfakes, impact, 46
Deep leadership, focus, 51
DeepMind (Google), 45
"Deep Work," 36
Deere, John, 108–109
Deglobalization, politics, 28
"Dieselgate," 179
Differences, 163
Digitalization, 27
"Disrupt and grow" mindsets,
     adoption, 122
Disruption, 8
   AI-driven disruption, 23
   industry disruption, 37–38
   initiation, 37
   leveraging, 27
   management, 108
   meaning, 16–17
   norm, 17–18, 171–173
   risk/change/opportunity, 181
   upside, 6–7, 12, 15, 20, 254
Distinct Elements of Trust and
     Autonomy (DELTAs),
     unlocking, 153
Divergence, 163
Divergent thinking, 163
Diversity, 164
   issue, 162–163
Diversity and Inclusion Index
     (Refinitv), 164

Djokovic, Novak (strengths), 172
DNA sequencing, 17
Downside surprises, protection, 105
DPD, AI chatbot problem, 47
Drucker, Peter, 39
Dual purpose, 58–59
D Word, mentioning
(avoidance), 16–17

E
Eames, Charles, 145
Economic Intelligence Unit, 120
Economies of scale, 38
Edmondson, Amy, 67
Emails, sending/receiving
(EarthWeb results), 175
Embedded Everywhere phase
(AI), 45–46
Embedded phase (AI), 42–43
Emotional burnout, suffering, 55
Emotional underload, 55
Empathy (bureaucratic BS
counterstrategy), 77
Employees, overmanagement/
underleading, 94–95
Empowerment, 149
Energy storage, 17
Engine No. 1 (activist investor), 12
Enshittification, 68
Ettarh, Fobazi, 143
Evolution, 28–29
embracing, 96
Excellence, ecosystem, 145
Excitement phase (AI), 42–43, 61
Execution certainty, 68, 110–111
Experimentation phase (AI), 44, 61
Experiment phase (AI), 42–43
Extreme ownership, 72–74

F
Failure
fear, 83
history, 81–84

learning, 82–83
reimagination problem, 79–81
Fear-focused leadership, 159
Fear of Becoming Obsolete
(FOBO), 68
Fear of Missing Out (FOMO),
3, 51, 115
Feedback, gathering, 151
Feedback sandwiches, 148–149
Feynman, Richard, 14
Forever Beta, 18, 40
Fragmented control, 38
Frances-White, Deborah, 15
Frei, Frances, 91
Friedman, Milton, 117, 119–120
From Action I Learn (FAIL), 84–87
Frontier leadership, 180–185
Future, regaining, 7
Future-fit, 59
Future-maker, 60–61
Future readiness, 39
Future-readiness, 92–93
Future readiness
challenges, 60
skills, 58, 176–177
Future-ready mindsets, 7–14

G
Galbraith, John Kenneth, 189
Galloway, Scott, 40–41
Gates, Bill, 36, 88
GatesNotes, 36
Geim, Andre, 85
Gemini, 28
General Electric, market
capitalization, 109
Generative AI (GenAI)
speed/impact, 34
testing, 44
usage, 8–9
Gensler, Gary, 14
Geopolitical risk, 4
Geopolitical Supercycle, 19

Ghosting, rise, 49, 53
Gibson, William, 42
Gloat (AI-powered talent
        marketplace provider), 55
Global economic
        downturn, 184–185
Global Financial Crisis, 16–17
Global labor supply problems, 28
Global pandemic, impact, 11
Global workforce, impact, 59
"Godlike technology," 51
GRANOLAS, impact, 9–10
Grant, Adam, 159
Gratton, Lynda, 146–147
Great Depression, 17, 183
Great Resignation, The, 10
Gretzky, Wayne, 157
Growth
    pathways, reimagining, 1235
    rates, maintenance, 106
    sameness, problem, 116
Gulden, Bjørn, 155

H
Hack Future Lab, 28
    estimates, 43, 111, 126, 140
    findings, 24–25, 57–58, 71
    research, 7, 22, 56, 93, 142
"Half-Life of Everything," 69
Hamel, Gary, 73
Hansen, Morten, 52
Harari, Yuval, 24
Harding, Verity, 45
Hawking, Stephen, 70
Headline risks
    clarity, 20
    noise, separation, 120
Heatherwick, Thomas, 21–22
Hemingway, Ernest, 6
High-velocity, high-quality
        decisions, strength, 76
Hinton, Geoffrey, 34
Holdfast Collective, 118

Holmes, Elizabeth, 141
Homo sapiens, 23
How We Grow (scalability), 154–157
    unlocking, questions, 156–157
How We Work (agility), 149–153
Huang, Jensen, 80
*Humanise: A Maker's Guide to
        Building Our World*
        (Heatherwick), 21
Humanity
    AI, matching, 54–55
    diminishment, 53
Human-led cultures, impact, 182
Human lives, improvement, 48
*Humanocracy: Creating Organizations
        as Amazing as the People
        Inside Them* (Hamel/
        Zanini), 73
Humans
    irrationality/unpredictability, 27
    trust, 137–139
Human-technology nexus, 175–177
Human-to-machine collaborative
        teamwork, 8
Human Trust Agenda, 158
Hybrid Paradox, 10
Hybrid Paradox (Klotz), 10

I
Identity, 143–145
IKEA, revenue forecasting, 93
Improv Handbook (Frances-White/
        Salinsky), 15
Incrementalism, 52
Industrial Age, 63, 70
    thinking
        antidote, 178–179
        cessation, 69
Industrial Revolution, witness, 17
Industry
    convergence, 7, 9–10
    disruption, 37–38
Inflation Reduction Act, 13

Ingram, Amy, 33
Inner attention, 53
Innovation platforms, 24
   convergence, 17–18
Innovator's Dilemma: When New
     Technologies Cause Great
     Firms to Fail
     (Christensen), 121
In-person meetings, increase, 50
Insilico Medicine, drug
     discovery, 36–37
Intelligence Age, 23, 43, 63, 70
   disruption, 25
Intelligent work, 73
Intergovernmental Panel on Climate
     Change (IPCC), 14,
     46, 116–117
Internal mobility, 57–58
International Panel on AI Safety
     (IPAIS), 14
Iron Age, 16
I-shaped workforce, 56

J
Jobs
   AI, impact (IMF research), 41
   automation, 5
Jobs, Steve, 41
John Deere
   leaders, self-perception, 111–112
   leadership team issues, 109–110
Jumbo (chain store), 47–48

K
Kahneman, Daniel, 54
Key Behavior Indicators (KBIs),
     adoption, 61–62
Key Performance Indicators
     (KPIs), 72, 127
Khosrowshahi, Dara, 89
King, Billie Jean (BJK), 19
Kletskassa (chat checkout), 47
Klotz, Anthony, 10

Knowledge
   answers, 14
   gap, closure, 19
   half-life, 69
   information, connection, 174
Kondo, Marie, 73
Kurzweil, Ray, 45–46

L
Labor supply problems, 28
Lagarde, Christine, 83–84
Large language models (LLMs), 37
   training, 46
Leaders
   change, 33–34
   competition, 12
   decision fatigue, 152
   distraction levels, 5
   institutional bias, 140
   overconfidence, replacement, 14
   requirement, 6
   study, 140–141
   uncertain times, 6
Leadership
   AI, matching, 54–55
   attention, issues, 50–54
   ballot, relationship, 5–7
   breakdown, 135
   complication/messiness, 19
   conformity mindsets, 11
   deep leadership, focus, 51
   dehumanization, 44–45
   evolution, 108
   fear-focused leadership, 159
   frontier leadership, 180–185
   logic, 35–36
   mindset, 69, 125
   models, 19
   momentum source, 56–57
   nutritional value, 21–30
   reimagining, 26
   strategies, models, 5
   style

description, 21–22
evolution, 95
tax, 74
trust-based leadership, metrics
  (usage), 160
value chain, rethinking, 172
Leaders of courage, need, 127
Leading, trust (usage), 159–160
Learning, 68–71
  discovery/failing, relationship, 82
LEGO, vision/strategic
      courage, 123–124
Lessons, learning, 152–153
Liquid Death, tagline, 11
Listening
  mindset, adoption, 160–162
  strength, 162
London Interdisciplinary School
      (LIS), impact, 56
Long-term sustainable value,
      creation, 119–120
Lovelace, Ada, 42
Low-value task, automation, 63
Lyft, 3

M
Machiavellian principles, 90–91
Mantel, Hillary, 3
Manual processes, 74
Mazzucato, Mariana, 48
Meeting-free days, usage, 52
Meetings, problems, 93
Megatrends, shift, 125
Messaging apps, impact, 50
Meta-anxiety, 138
Meta stock, increase/growth, 27
Metaverse, 39, 43
Microsoft, outperformance,
      105–106
Microsoft, Apple, Amazon, NVIDIA,
      Meta, Alphabet
      (MAANMA), 9–10
Milestones, creation, 125

"Million House Challenge," 112
Milton, Trevor, 141
Mindset
  advantage, 120–122
  change, 50–51
  shift, 108
Minimum Viable Idea (MVI), 18
Minsky, Marvin, 42–43
Mission Trust, 71
Mistral AI, 40
Moore's Law, 11
Murakami, Haruki, 184–185
Murthy, Vivek, 47
Must-do priorities, 5
MycoWorks, 156–157

N
Nadella, Satya, 25
Naisbitt, John, 49
Narrow ambition, 68
Netflix, share value (drop), 38
Neurons, connections
      (building), 68–69
Newport, Cal, 36
Nineteen Eighty-Four (Orwell), 139
No-fail trust, basis, 160
No Malice/No Mercy
      (Galloway), 40–41
Non-fungible tokens (NFTs), 39
"No regrets" mantra, 183
Norges Bank Investment
      Management (NBIM),
      sovereign wealth fund
      management, 25–26
No strategy, 52
Novoselov, Kostya, 85

O
Obama, Barack, 149
Objectives and Key Results (OKRs),
      77, 92–93, 126
Obsolescence, 108
  fear, 178–179

OpenAI, 4
  GPT store, plan, 104
  lawsuit, 13
Opportunity, expansion/
      shrinking, 114
Optimism, absence, 24
Organizational culture, 126
Organizational speed, increase, 69
Organizations, truth decay, 136
Ørsted (DONG Energy), beyonder
      role, 123–126
  beta testing, 126
Ørsted, Hans Christian, 124
Orwell, George, 139
Other attention, 53
Outer attention, 53–54

P
Palantir Technologies (data
      analytics), 37
Paranoia, reaction, 33–34
Patagonia, 119–120
  founding, 116–117
Patagonia Purpose Trust, 118
Performance
  annual reviews, 119
  resilience, sustaining, 113–114
Performance gaps, 68, 105
"Perma Crises" ("Poly Crises"), 121
Personalization, 10–11
Pichai, Sundar, 43
Possibility zone, 106
Post-AI Guiding Principles, 45
Post-industrial AI-centric economy,
      demands, 10
Poulsen, Henrik, 123–124
Predictive algorithms, usage, 45–46
Present forward thinking, leader
      rejection, 58
Proactive resilience, 68
Problems, crises (relationship), 147
Problem-solving, support, 44
Productive failure, 84–85

Productivity
  paradox, 49
  pressure, increase, 50
Project December, 6

R
Race to Reskill, 10
Radical receptivity, 125
Reactive inside-out teams,
      impact, 161
Reactive resilience, 68
Regulations, 13–14
Re-industrialization, 109–110
Reinvention, characterization, 176
Re-perception, 83–84
Resilience dividend, 172
Reskilling Revolution, 42
Resource allocation, 72
Re-thinking, 173
Return on courage, 112–115
Return on Intelligence, 73–74
Reynolds, Elizabeth, 109
*Right Side of Wrong: The Science
      of Failing Well*
      (Edmondson), 67
Ripple intelligence, 161
Risk, 26–27
  attitude, 181
Robotics, 17
Role-modeling, usage, 160
Roubini, Nouriel, 16
Rubber band effect, 177–179

S
Sachs, Oliver, 12
Sagan, Carl, 60
Sagan, Scott, 120
Salinsky, Tom, 15
Sameness, risk, 115
Scandals, impact, 28–29
Schumpeter, Joseph, 38, 108
Self-managing teams,
      networks, 107

Shallow leadership, time
    allotment, 74
"Shallow Work," 36
Shared purpose, 144
Shareholder, focus (cessation), 119
Shopify, meetings (changes), 93
Short-term thinking, avoidance, 153
Shoshin, 63
Silence breakers, 89–90
Silicon Valley Bank (SVB),
    collapse, 28–29
Similarity, strategies models, 5
Simple, Eliminate, Automate, or
    Outsource (SEAO), 77, 79
Simplicity Sprint, usage, 151
Skills, half-life, 69
Social media, impact, 51
Society of Mind Theory, 42–43
Somebody Else's Problem
    (SEP), 6, 89
Sora (OpenAI), 37
SpaceX, aerospace
    revolution, 180–181
Speed, importance, 111–112
Spiro, Rand, 41–42
Stakeholders, empowerment, 77
Stoics, perspective, 4, 81
Stone Age, 16
Stora Enso, leaders (impact), 26–27
Stripe, 38
Success
    fallacy, 179–180
    headlines, achievement
        (aim), 172–173
Suleyman, Mustafa, 46
Supply chains, 38
Sustain (bureaucratic BS
    counterstrategy), 78–79
Sustainability, 27
Sutherland, Rory, 54–55, 176
Swartz, Jeff, 55
Sweet, Julie, 61
Swift, Taylor (impact), 114–115

Synergies, creation, 8
Syntax error message, 6

T
Tailwind, 12, 108
Talent
    currency unit, 10
    demand, 59
    ecosystems, 160
    scarcity, 5, 7, 10, 56, 141
    shortages, 4
Talent-crushing bureaucracy, 5
Tangen, Nicola, 26
Tang Ping, 6
Taylor, Frederick, 22
Teachability, 25
Technology
    change, 173–175
    client, partnering, 176–177
    disruption, 103–104
    innovation, 109–110
    runaway technology, impact, 175
    speed, learning, 145
    Supercycle, 35
Techno sapiens, 23
Terkel, Studs, 149
Third Point (activist investor), 12
TikTok (ByteDance), 38
Toffler, Alvin, 68
Torrance, Ellis Paul, 122
Toxic culture, unlearning, 87–91
"Tragedy of the horizon,"
    avoidance, 119
Triple attention, fortification, 53–54
Trust, 28–29, 136, 163–165
    breaches, 140
    certainty, 135
    clarifier role, 137
    cultivation, 86–87
    damage, 61
    decay, 139–141
    ecosystem, 144, 160
    energizer role, 138

Trust (*continued*)
    future, 157–164
    issues, 158
    mindset, 142–145
        identity/agility/scalability,
            relationship, 143
        signs, 145
    "no" strategy, 138–139
    requirement, 158
    simplifier role, 137–138
Trust-based cultures, impact, 182
Trust-based leadership, metrics
        (usage), 160
Trust-focused companies, 159
Truth
    decay, 136
    essence, 149
T-shaped workforce, 56

U
Uber, 3
    culture, 87–89
    missteps, 90–91
Ubuntu, potential, 56
Uncertainty, reduction, 84–85
Unknown, relationship
        (nurturing), 7
Unlearning, 24–25, 70
    agility/humility,
        equivalence, 95–96
    answer, 92–95
    courage, 20
    cycle, 67
    future, 68–71
    importance, 71–72
    learning form, 68
    quarterly challenge, 77–78
    reflection/feed-forward, 78–79
Unlearning Champions,
        recognition/celebration, 78
Upside
    answer, 18–20
    choice, 17–18

V
Value Act (activist investor), 12
Value chain disintermediation, 82
Velocity, focus, 52
Vertical power, 38
Virtual meetings,
        increase, 50
Vocational awe, 143
Voice cloning, impact, 45

W
Warm technology, 48–49
Waymo, 3–14
Web 3.0, 39
WeWork, growth, 28–29
Who We Are (Trust Mindset
        dimension), 143–145
Willful contrarianism,
        115–120, 178–179
Wilson, Edward O., 51
Wirecard, collapse, 141
Wisdom gap, 174
Work
    anti-agile characteristic, 62
    rethinking, 153
Work Disrupted: Opportunity,
        Growth, and Opportunity in
        The Accelerated Future
        (Swartz), 55
Working: People Talk About What They
        Do All Day and How They
        Feel About What They Do
        (Terkel), 149
World Uncertainty Index,
        measure, 120

Y
Yuk Hui, 7

Z
Zanini, Michele, 73
Zombie leadership, 4, 54, 148
    avoidance, 92